Getting Started with RStudio

John Verzani

O'REILLY®

Beijing · Cambridge · Farnham · Köln · Sebastopol · Tokyo

Getting Started with RStudio

by John Verzani

Copyright © 2011 John Verzani. All rights reserved.
Printed in the United States of America.

Published by O'Reilly Media, Inc., 1005 Gravenstein Highway North, Sebastopol, CA 95472.

O'Reilly books may be purchased for educational, business, or sales promotional use. Online editions are also available for most titles (*http://my.safaribooksonline.com*). For more information, contact our corporate/institutional sales department: (800) 998-9938 or *corporate@oreilly.com*.

Editor: Mike Loukides
Production Editor: Kristen Borg
Proofreader: O'Reilly Production Services

Cover Designer: Karen Montgomery
Interior Designer: David Futato
Illustrator: Robert Romano

Revision History for the First Edition:
   2011-09-15 First release
   2012-03-20 Second release
See *http://oreilly.com/catalog/errata.csp?isbn=9781449309039* for release details.

ISBN: 978-1-449-30903-9

[LSI]

1332254129

Table of Contents

Preface

Conventions Used in This Book

The following typographical conventions are used in this book:

Italic
> Indicates new terms, URLs, email addresses, filenames, and file extensions.

`Constant width`
> Used for program listings, as well as within paragraphs to refer to program elements such as variable or function names, databases, data types, environment variables, statements, and keywords.

`Constant width bold`
> Shows commands or other text that should be typed literally by the user.

`Constant width italic`
> Shows text that should be replaced with user-supplied values or by values determined by context.

 This icon signifies a tip, suggestion, or general note.

 This icon indicates a warning or caution.

Using Code Examples

This book is here to help you get your job done. In general, you may use the code in this book in your programs and documentation. You do not need to contact us for permission unless you're reproducing a significant portion of the code. For example, writing a program that uses several chunks of code from this book does not require permission. Selling or distributing a CD-ROM of examples from O'Reilly books does require permission. Answering a question by citing this book and quoting example code does not require permission. Incorporating a significant amount of example code from this book into your product's documentation does require permission.

We appreciate, but do not require, attribution. An attribution usually includes the title, author, publisher, and ISBN. For example: "*Getting Started with RStudio* by John Verzani (O'Reilly). Copyright 2011 John Verzani, 978-1-449-30903-9."

If you feel your use of code examples falls outside fair use or the permission given above, feel free to contact us at *permissions@oreilly.com*.

Safari® Books Online

Safari·› Safari Books Online is an on-demand digital library that lets you easily
Books Online search over 7,500 technology and creative reference books and videos to find the answers you need quickly.

With a subscription, you can read any page and watch any video from our library online. Read books on your cell phone and mobile devices. Access new titles before they are available for print, and get exclusive access to manuscripts in development and post feedback for the authors. Copy and paste code samples, organize your favorites, download chapters, bookmark key sections, create notes, print out pages, and benefit from tons of other time-saving features.

O'Reilly Media has uploaded this book to the Safari Books Online service. To have full digital access to this book and others on similar topics from O'Reilly and other publishers, sign up for free at *http://my.safaribooksonline.com*.

How to Contact Us

Please address comments and questions concerning this book to the publisher:

> O'Reilly Media, Inc.
> 1005 Gravenstein Highway North
> Sebastopol, CA 95472
> 800-998-9938 (in the United States or Canada)
> 707-829-0515 (international or local)
> 707-829-0104 (fax)

We have a web page for this book, where we list errata, examples, and any additional information. You can access this page at:

http://shop.oreilly.com/product/0636920021278.do

To comment or ask technical questions about this book, send email to:

bookquestions@oreilly.com

For more information about our books, courses, conferences, and news, see our website at *http://www.oreilly.com*.

Find us on Facebook: *http://facebook.com/oreilly*

Follow us on Twitter: *http://twitter.com/oreillymedia*

Watch us on YouTube: *http://www.youtube.com/oreillymedia*

Content Updates

March 20, 2012

- New material on projects and the use of version control with RStudio was added to "Organizing Activities with Projects" on page 73.
- Updated many figures to reflect interface of RStudio version 0.95
- Made many copy edits to fix errors and adjust for changes introduced by version 0.95. Special thanks to Josh Paulson for a careful reading and many useful suggestions.
- Example files have been loaded to the book's catalog page, and can be downloaded here: *http://examples.oreilly.com/0636920021278*.

CHAPTER 1

Overview, Installation

This book introduces users to the RStudio™ Integrated Development Environment (IDE) for using and programming R, the widely used open-source statistical computing environment. RStudio is a separate open-source project that brings many powerful coding tools together into an intuitive, easy-to-learn interface. RStudio runs in all major platforms (Windows, Mac, Linux) and through a web browser (using the server installation). This book should appeal to newer R users, students who want to explore the interface to get the most out of R, and long-time R users looking for a more modern development environment.

RStudio is periodically released as a stable version, and has daily releases in between. This book describes the stable release 0.95, which introduced many new features to RStudio: projects for organizing code, powerful code navigation tools, and integration with two popular version control systems.

We will begin with a quick overview of R and IDEs before diving into RStudio.

What is R?

R is an open-source software environment for statistical computing and graphics. R compiles and runs on Windows, Mac OS X, and numerous UNIX platforms (such as Linux). For most platforms, R is distributed in binary format for ease of installation. The R software project was first started by Robert Gentleman and Ross Ihaka. The language was very much influenced by the S language, which was originally developed at Bell Laboratories by John Chambers and colleagues. Since then, with the direction and talents of R's core development team, R has evolved into the lingua franca for statistical computations in many disciplines of academia and various industries.

R is much more than just its core language. It has a worldwide repository system, the Comprehensive R Archive Network (CRAN)—*http://cran.r-project.org*—for user-contributed add-on packages to supplement the base distribution. As of 2011, there were more than 3,000 such packages hosted on CRAN and numerous more on other sites. In total, R currently has functionality to address an enormous range of problems and still has room to grow.

R is designed around its core scripting language but also allows integration with compiled code written in C, C++, Fortran, Java, etc., for computationally intensive tasks or for leveraging tools provided for other languages.

What is an IDE?

R, like other programming languages, is extended (or developed) through user-written functions. An integrated development environment (IDE), such as RStudio, is designed to facilitate such work. In addition, unlike many other statistical software packages in which a graphical user interface is employed, a typical user interacts with R primarily through the command line. An IDE for R then must also include a means for issuing commands interactively. R is not unique in this respect, and IDEs for interactive scientific programming languages have matured to include features such as:

- A console for issuing commands.
- Source-code editor; at its core, development involves the act of programming, and this task is inevitably done with a source-code editor. Such editors have been around for some time now, and expectations for editors are now quite demanding. A typical set of expectations includes:
    - A rich set of keyboard shortcuts
    - Automatic source-code formatting, assistance with parentheses, keyword highlighting
    - Code folding and easy navigation through a file and among files
    - Context-sensitive assistance
    - Interfaces for compiling or running of software
    - Project-management features
    - Debugging assistance
    - Integration with report-writing tools
- Object browsers; in interactive use, a user's workspace includes variables that have been defined. An object browser allows the user to identify quickly the type and values for each such variable.
- Object editors; from an object browser, a means to inspect or edit objects is typically provided.

- Integration with the underlying documentation.
- Plot-management tools.

Some existing IDEs for R are listed in Table 1-1.

Table 1-1. Some existing IDEs for R

Name	Platforms	Description
ESS	All	ESS (*http://ess.r-project.org*) is a powerful and commonly used interface for R that integrates the venerable Emacs editor with R. There are numerous conveniences, but some find that it is difficult to learn and has an old-school feel, which precludes adoption.
Eclipse	All	The open-source StatET plugin (*http://www.walware.de/goto/statet*) turns Eclipse, a Java-based multipurpose IDE, into a full-featured IDE for R.
SciViews	All	An R API and extension for the Komodo code editor.
JGR	All	Java-based editor that interfaces with R through the rJava and JRI packages. The Deducer package adds a suite of data analysis tools.
Tinn-R	Windows	An extension for the Tinn editor that allows integration with an underlying R process.
Notepad++	Windows	With the NpptoR extension allows the Notepad++ editor to interact with an R process.
RGui	Windows	The Windows GUI for R (the default interface) has some of the features of an IDE.
R.app	Mac OS X	Like the Windows GUI, provides the basic features of an IDE.

Why RStudio?

In its short existence, the RStudio project already provides nearly all the desired features for an IDE in a novel way, making it easier and more productive to use R. Further, new features are being added all the time. Some current highlights are:

- The main components of an IDE are all nicely integrated into a four-pane layout that includes a console for interactive R sessions, a tabbed source-code editor to organize a project's files, and tabbed panes within notebooks to organize less central components.
- The source-code editor is easy to use, feature-rich, has excellent code-navigation features, and is well-integrated into the built-in console.
- The console and source-code editor are tightly linked to R's internal help system through tab completion and the help page viewer component.
- The project feature make it easy to organize different workflows. Setting up different projects is a snap, and switching between them is even easier.
- RStudio provides many convenient and easy-to-use administrative tools for managing packages, the workspace, files, and more.

- The IDE is available for the three main operating systems *and* can be run through a web browser for remote access.
- RStudio is much easier to learn than Emacs/ESS, easier to configure and install than Eclipse/StatET, has a much better editor than JGR, is better organized than Sciviews, and unlike Notepad++ and RGui, is available on more platforms than just Windows.

The RStudio program can be run on the desktop or through a web browser. The desktop version is available for Windows, Mac OS X, and Linux platforms and behaves similarly across all platforms, with minor differences for keyboard shortcuts.

To support so many platforms, RStudio leverages numerous existing web technologies in its design. For the desktop applications, it cleverly displays them within an industry standard HTML widget provided by *Qt* (a cross-platform application and UI framework) to create a desktop application. Consequently, R users can have a feature-rich and consistent programming environment for R their way—desktop- or web-based. Web-based usage is done through a trusted server within a department or organization (though a "cloud" service may be forthcoming).

RStudio is the brainchild of J. J. Allaire, who, with his brother, previously had tremendous success developing the influential ColdFusion IDE and scripting language for web development. Allaire is currently joined by the very able Joseph Cheng, Joshua Paulson, and Paul DiCristina. In the short time that their initial beta has been available, they have proven to be very responsive to user input. RStudio is under active development. As such, elements discussed in this book may be changed by the time you are reading it. Sorry...but you'll likely be better off with the new feature than my description of the old one.

Like R, RStudio is an open-source project. Its stated goal—which it is already meeting —is "...to develop a powerful tool that supports the practices and techniques required for creating trustworthy, high-quality analysis." The codebase is released under the AGPLv3 license and is available from GitHub (*https://github.com/rstudio/rstudio*). RStudio is built on top of many other open-source projects. Most visible of these are *GWT*, Google's Web Toolkit; *Qt*, the graphical toolkit of Nokia; and *Ace*, the JavaScript code editor (*http://ace.ajax.org*). Other leveraged projects are listed in RStudio's About dialog. The bulk of the code is written in C++ and Java, the language for working with GWT.

Using RStudio

We will reverse things slightly by beginning with the process of starting RStudio, and postpone any installation issues for a bit. As RStudio can be used from the desktop or through a server, there are two ways of starting it.

Desktop Version

For the desktop version, RStudio is started like most other applications. In Figure 1-1, we see the application running under a version of Windows. There it was started by clicking on the menu item left after installation. For Mac OS X users, one clicks on the RStudio icon in the Applications list. For Linux users, the command `rstudio` will open the window. It may also be installed with a menu item, as is done with Ubuntu, where it appears under `Programming`.

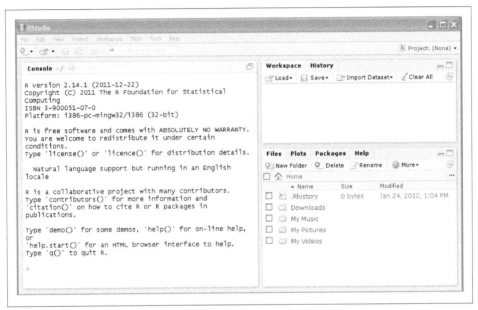

Figure 1-1. RStudio on initial startup; the main interface has four panes (one hidden in this screenshot), an application toolbar, and in some cases, a menu bar

In Figure 1-1 we see three main panes: the `Console`, which should look familiar to any R user; a tabbed `Workspace` pane (with no items, as the initial workspace is empty) and the `History` interface. The latter two are part of notebooks that can contain multiple panes. The `Source` pane, or code editor, is not open in the screenshot, as no files are open for editing or viewing.

Server Version

Starting the server version requires one to know the appropriate URL for the resource. We used a local URL for this book, but the real value comes from using RStudio as a resource on the wider internet. When accessing RStudio, one must first authenticate. The basic screen to do so looks like Figure 1-2. Authentication depends on the server, but the default is to authenticate against the user accounts on the machine, so the web adminstrator should have provided a secure means to access RStudio.

Figure 1-2. *Login screen for the server version of RStudio*

Once authenticated, the basic layout looks similar to that of the desktop version—compare the basic elements of Figure 1-1 to Figure 1-3 to see this.

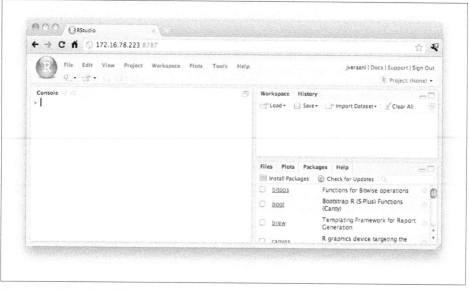

Figure 1-3. *Screenshot of RStudio startup run through a web browser; here, the Source component is hidden, as no files are currently being edited*

 When using the server version, only one instance per user may be opened. If a new session is started—on a different machine, or even if just in a different tab of the same browser—the old one is disconnected and a notification issued.

Which Workspace?

When R is started, it follows this process:

- R is started in the working directory.
- If present, the *.Rprofile* file's commands are executed.
- If present, the *.RData* file is loaded.
- Other actions described in `?Startup` are followed.

When R quits, a user is queried to "Save workspace image?" When the workspace is saved it writes the contents to an *.RData* file, so that when R is restarted the workspace can persist between sessions. (One can also initiate this with `save.image`.)

This process allows R users to place commands they desire to run in every session in an *.Rprofile* file, and to have per directory *.RData* files, so that different global workspaces can be used for different projects.

Projects

RStudio provides a very useful "project" feature that allows a user to switch quickly between projects ("Organizing Activities with Projects" on page 73). Each project may have different working directories, workspaces, and collection of files in the `Source` component. The current project name is listed on the far right of the main application toolbar in a combobox that allows one to switch between open projects, open an existing project, or create a new project.

Which R?

RStudio does not require a special version of R to run, as long as it is a fairly modern one (R 2.11.1 or later). It will work with binary versions from CRAN or user-compiled versions. As such, when RStudio starts up, it must be able to locate a version of R, which could possibly reside in many different places. Usually RStudio just finds the right one, but one can bypass the search process. The online document at *http:// www.rstudio.org/docs/advanced/versions_of_r* details how to specify which R installation to use. In short, it depends on the underlying operating system. For Windows desktop users, it can be specified in the Options dialog (see "The Options Dialog" on page 9), or chosen if the Ctrl key is held on startup. For Linux and Mac OS X users, one can set an environment variable, as seen here:

```
$ export RSTUDIO_WHICH_R=/usr/local/bin/R
```

Web-based users really don't have a choice, as this is determined by who configures the server.

Layout of the Components

The RStudio interface consists of several main components sitting below a top-level toolbar and menu bar. Although this placement can be customized, the default layout utilizes four main panes in the following positions:

- In the upper left is a Source browser pane for editing files (see "Source Code Editor" on page 61) or viewing some data sets. In Figure 1-3 this is not visible, as that session had no files open.
- In the lower left is a Console for interacting with an R process (see Chapter 3).
- In the upper right are tabs for a Workspace browser (see the section "Workspace Browser" on page 35) and a History browser (see the section "Command History" on page 33).
- In the lower right are tabbed panes for interacting with the Files ("The File Browser" on page 69), Plots ("Graphics in RStudio" on page 43), Packages ("Package Maintenance" on page 70), and Help system components ("The Help Page Viewer" on page 39). If the facilities are present, an additional tab for version control ("Version Control with RStudio" on page 75) is presented.

The Console pane is somewhat privileged: it is always visible, and it has a title bar. For the other components, their tab serves as a title bar. These panes have page-specific toolbars (perhaps more than one)—which in the case of the Source pane are also context-specific.

The user may change the default dimensions for each of the panes, as follows. There is an adjustable divider appearing in the middle of the interface between the left and right sides that allows the user to adjust the horizontal allocation of space. Furthermore, each side then has another divider to adjust the vertical space between its two panes. As well, the title bar of each pane has icons to shade a component, maximize a component vertically, or share the space.

Keyboard Shortcuts

One can easily switch between components using the mouse. As well, the View menu has subitems for this task. For power users, the keyboard shortcuts listed in Table 1-2 are useful. (A full list of keyboard shortcuts is available through the Help > Keyboard Shortcuts menu item.)

Table 1-2. *Keyboard shortcuts for navigation between major components*

Description	Windows & Linux	Mac
Move cursor to Source Editor	Ctrl+1	Ctrl+1
Move cursor to Console	Ctrl+2	Ctrl+2
Show workspace	Ctrl+3	Ctrl+3
Show history	Ctrl+4	Ctrl+4
Show files	Ctrl+5	Ctrl+5
Show plots	Ctrl+6	Ctrl+6
Show packages	Ctrl+7	Ctrl+7
Show help	Ctrl+8	Ctrl+8
Show Git/SVN	Ctrl+9	Ctrl+9
Shell	Ctrl+Shift+H	Cmd+Shift+H

The Options Dialog

RStudio preferences are adjusted through the Options dialog. There are five panels for this dialog to adjust: general properties, editing properties (Figure 3-4), appearance properties, pane layout (Figure 1-4), and version control (requires additional support tools to be installed).

The pane layout allows the user to determine which panes go in which corners, and, for the supplemental panes (not the Console or Source editor), where those pane's tabs appear. One modifies a placement simply by adjusting a combobox, or by checking one of the checkboxes. In Figure 1-4, the choices put the code editor on the right, the console in the upper right, and the file browser on the upper left. There are many examples of pane placement on *http://rstudio.org/screenshots/*.

The appearance panel of the options dialog allows one to set the default font size and modify the theme for the editing in the console or source-code editor. This book uses the default *TextMate* theme for its screenshots.

Installing RStudio

Installing RStudio is usually a straightforward process.

First, RStudio requires a working, relatively modern R installation. If that is not already present, then one should consult *http://cran.r-project.org* to learn how to install R for the given operating system. For Windows and Mac OS X, one can simply download a self-installing binary; for Linux, installation varies. For the Debian distribution (including Ubuntu), the R system can be installed using the regular package-management tools. Of course, as R is open source, one can also compile and install it using the source code.

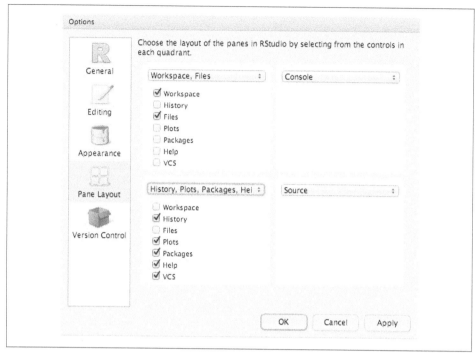

Figure 1-4. Pane preference dialog for adjusting component layout

The RStudio package is available for download from *http://www.rstudio.org/download/*. There is a choice between a Desktop version and a Server version. The Desktop version is appropriate for single-user use. The files come in a common format for binary installation (e.g., *exe*, *dmg*, *deb*, or *rpm*). One downloads the file and installs it as any other program.

For those searching out the latest features, follow the link on *http://www.rstudio.org/download/daily* to get the binaries for the most recent (but not necessarily stable) build.

Installing a server version requires more work and care. Some directions are given at *http://rstudio.org/docs/*.

One can also install RStudio from its source code. A link for the source "tarball" for the current stable version appears on the appropriate download page. For the adventurous, the latest development build files are available from *https://github.com/rstudio/rstudio*. Installation details are in the INSTALL file accompanying the source code. The same source is used to compile both the Desktop and Server version.

As RStudio depends on some of the latest features of many moving parts, such as GWT, there can be issues with compiling from the source. The support forums (*http://support.rstudio.org/*) are an excellent place to find specific answers to any issues.

Logging

RStudio creates hidden files for itself to store information, including logging information. When there are issues at startup, the log can be consulted for direction as to what is going wrong.

For desktop users, the log directory is either *~/.rstudio-desktop/log* for Mac and Linux users; or for Windows users, *%localappdata%\RStudio-Desktop\log* (Windows Vista and 7) or *%USERPROFILE%\Local Settings\Application Data\RStudio-Desktop\log* for XP.

In the application's menu bar, the `Help > Diagnostics` item can be used to find the log files.

Updating RStudio

Updating RStudio is also straightforward.

To see if an update is available, the `Help > Check for Updates` menu item will open a dialog with update information.

If an update is available, one can stop RStudio, install the new version, then restart. RStudio writes session information to the user's home directory (e.g., to the file *~/.rstudio-desktop*). This will persist between upgrades.

CHAPTER 2

Case Study: Data Cleaning

Now that we know how to start RStudio, let's dive in. We'll begin with a blow-by-blow account of a sample data analysis for which we read in some data, clean it up, then format it for further study. We deliberately chose an example that will take us on some detours, as the point of the exercise is to show how many of RStudio's features can be used during the process to speed the task along. We will postpone for now an example of the "development" aspect of RStudio.

The data set we look at here comes from a colleague, and contains records from a psychology experiment on a colony of naked mole rats. The experimenter is interested in both the behavior of each naked mole rat in time and the social aspect of the colony as a whole.

Each rat wears an RFID chip that allows the researcher to track its motion. The experiment consists of 15 chambers (bubbles) in a linear arrangement separated by 14 tubes. Each tube has a gate with a sensor. When a mole rat passes through the tube, the time and gate are recorded. Unfortunately, gates can be missed, and the recording device can erroneously replicate values, so the raw data must be cleaned up.

This data comes to us in rich-text format (*rtf*). This quasi text-based format is a bit unusual for data transfer but presumably is used by the recording apparatus. We will see that this format has some idiosyncrasies that will require us to work a little harder than we might normally do to read data into an RStudio session, but don't worry, RStudio is up to the task.

Our first step is to copy the file into a directory named NMR. We are performing this analysis using the desktop version, so we simply copy the file the usual way after making a new directory. Had we been working through a server, we could have uploaded the file into a new directory using first the New Folder toolbar button, then the Upload toolbar button of the Files component.

Using Projects

To organize our work, we set up a new project (see the section "Organizing Activities with Projects" on page 73). RStudio allows us to compartmentalize our work into projects that have separate global workspaces and associated files and integrate seamlessly with version control systems. We easily navigate between projects using a selector (a combobox) in the main toolbar located in the upper-right corner. The same selector has an option to create a `New Project...`, which we choose. To create a new project, one fills in a project name and location, and if available, one can specify if version control is to be used.

When the project is created, the working directory is set. The title bar of the `Console` pane is updated, as are the contents of the `Files` component, which lists the files and subdirectories in a given directory. The `Files` pane resides by default in the lower-right corner. If it isn't showing, select its tab. In Figure 2-1, we see that our working directory contains our data file and a bookkeeping file written when RStudio created the package.

Figure 2-1. The Files browser shows files added when a new project is created

The `Files` browser pane is typical of RStudio's components. In addition to the main application toolbar, most components come with their own toolbar. In this case, the toolbar has buttons to add a new folder, delete selected files, etc. In addition, the `Files` component adds a second toolbar to facilitate the selection of files and navigation within directories.

Reading in a Data File

Clicking on the data file name in the file browser opens up a system text editor (Figure 2-2), allowing us to edit the file. For many text-based files, the file will open in RStudio's source-code editor. However, the actual editor employed depends on the extension and MIME type of the file. For *rtf* files, the underlying operating system's editor is used, which for Mac OS X is `textedit`. We can see that the data appears to

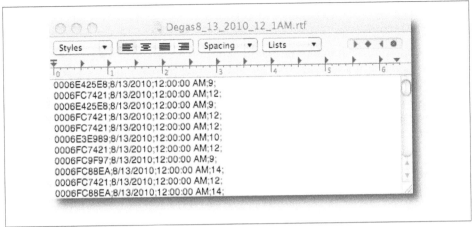

Figure 2-2. The rtf file is opened in an editor provided by the system, not by RStudio

have one line per record, with the values separated by semicolons. The fields are RFID, date, time, and gate number. This is basically comma-separated-value (CSV) data with a nonstandard separator.

However, although we rarely see *rtf* files, we know the `textedit` program of Mac OS X will likely render them using the markup for formatting, so perhaps there are some markup commands that need to be removed. To investigate, we make a copy of the data file, but store it instead with a *txt* extension. The `Files` component makes it easy to perform basic file operations such as this. To make a copy of a file, one selects the checkbox next to the file and invokes the `More > Copy…` menu item, as seen in Figure 2-3.

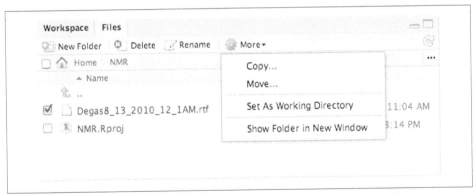

Figure 2-3. Copying files in the Files browser—the command acts on the checked file

We change the extension to *txt* and our file list is updated. (In general this can be a really bad practice, especially for binary files, though in this case we know *rtf* files can be viewed as plain text.) The displayed contents of the directory may also be refreshed by clicking the terminus on the path indicated by the links to the right of the house icon in the secondary toolbar; or the refresh icon on the far right of the component's main toolbar. Now, clicking on the *txt* file opens the file in RStudio's source-code editor as a text file (Figure 2-4).

The editor's status bar shows us the line and position of the cursor and, on the far right, that we are looking at a text file. We can now see that there is indeed a header (and, if we scroll down, a footer) wrapping our data. We highlight the header and then use the Delete key to remove this content from the file. We then scroll to the bottom of the file and remove a trailing brace. Afterwards, we click the Save toolbar button (the floppy-disk toolbar button, which is grayed out in the figure, as no changes have been made).

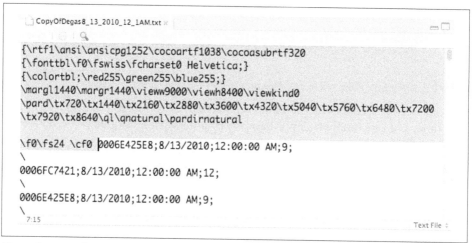

Figure 2-4. RStudio's code editor showing actual contents of our data file; we need to delete the rtf formatting before reading in

We now wish to read in the file using `read.csv`. RStudio provides an `Import Dataset` toolbar button under the `Workspace` component, which provides an interface that will handle most *csv* data, such as that exported from a spreadsheet. In this example though, we have a few idiosyncrasies that prevent its use. (This is a deliberate choice to show off some of RStudio's other features.)

So we head on over to the `Console` component to do the work. With the default pane arrangement the console is located on the left side (the lower-left pane if the editor is open). In R, one can't avoid the console, and RStudio's should look very familiar to any R user.

Tab Completion

At the console we create the command to call the `read.csv` function directly. This requires us to specify a few of its arguments, as we have a different separator, an odd character every other line, and no header. We will use the tab completion feature to assist us in filling in these values. This feature provides completion candidates for many different settings, allowing us in this case to recall quickly the names for lesser-used arguments.

First, we type `read.csv` in the console. Then we press the Tab key to bring up the tab completion dialog (Figure 2-5) for this function.

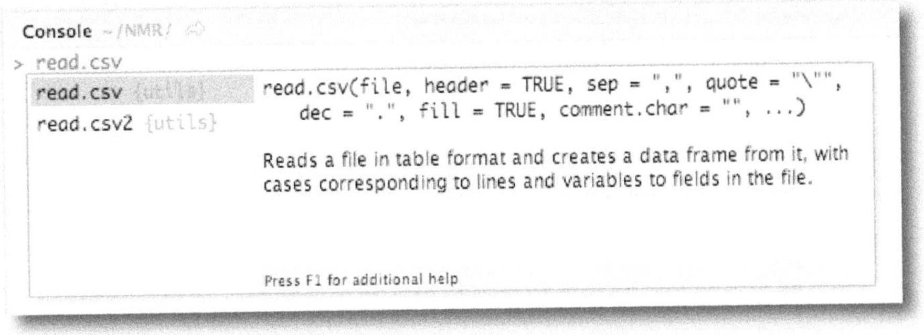

Figure 2-5. Tab completion dialog showing small snippet about the read.csv function from the function's help page

RStudio's tab completion dialog for a function nicely displays its arguments and a short description, gleaned from its help page (when available). In this example we see the `sep` argument is what we need to specify a semicolon for a separator, the `header` argument to specify a non-default header, and `comment.char` to skip the lines starting with a backslash.

The file name is the first argument. For file names (indicated by quotes), tab completion will fill in the file name, or, if more than one candidate is possible, provide a popup (Figure 2-6) to fill in the file. Here we type a left parentheses and double quote, and RStudio provides the matching values.

Figure 2-6. Tab-key completion for strings; a list of files is presented

We press the Tab key again to select the proposed completion value using our modified text file, not the original. We then add a comma and again press the Tab key. When the prompt is in a function body, the tab completion will prompt for function arguments. After entering our values, we have this command to issue (see also Figure 2-7, where the command is shown in the console):

```
> x <- read.csv("CopyOfDegas8_13_2010_12_1AM.txt", sep=";",
+ header=FALSE, comment.char="\\")
```

```
Console ~/NMR/
> x  <- read.csv("CopyOfDegas8_13_2010_12_1AM.txt", sep=";",
+ header=FALSE, comment.char="\\")
```

Figure 2-7. Command to read the "csv" file holding the data within the RStudio console

 The backslash argument for `command.char` is doubled, thereby escaping it. Failing to do this, the parser will use the backslash to escape the matching quote, getting the parser confused, as no matching quote will be found. Pressing the Escape key will terminate the continuation prompt so that the command can be fixed.

Workspace Component

The `Workspace` component lists the objects in the project's global workspace. In the default pane layout, this component is in the upper-right pane along with the `His tory` component. If this pane isn't raised, we simply click on its tab (or perform the keyboard shortcut Ctrl-3) to do so. After the data is read in, this component is updated to reflect the new object, in this case one named x (Figure 2-8). The associated icon for x shows it to be rectangular data. Clicking on x's row invokes the `View` function on x—in this case, opening the data viewer (Figure 2-9).

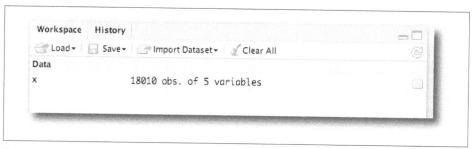

Figure 2-8. Workspace browser showing a data object x

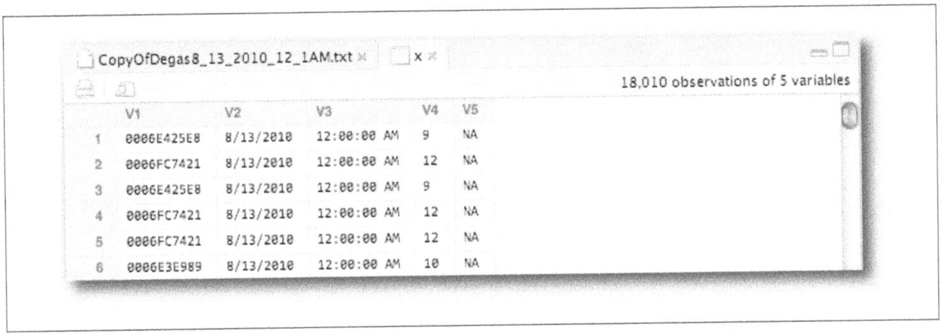

Figure 2-9. Data viewer window showing non-editable display of the x data frame

The data viewer shows us that we have an unnecessary fifth column of NA values, and that our variable names need improvement. Although the data viewer of RStudio does not yet support editing, R has many ways to manipulate rectangular data at the command line. For our two tasks we issue the following:

```
> x <- x[ , -5]
> names(x) <- c("RFID", "date", "time", "gate")
```

The view of x in the code-editor pane does not update from changes at the command line; rather, it is a snapshot. The Workspace component does reflect the current state of the variable, and reclicking on that will refresh the view.

Using the Right Class to Store Data

The data is time-series data, but the date and time are read in and stored by read.csv as factors, not times. R has many different classes for working with time-series data. In this case study we will look at two. The POSIXct class records time by the number of seconds since the beginning of 1970 and is useful for storing times in a data frame, such as x. We will use the coercion function as.POSIXct for this task. As this function isn't part of our daily repertoire, we call up its help page. Opening a help page can be done in the standard way: ?as.POSIXct (Figure 2-10).

Help pages are displayed in the Help pane, located by default in the lower-right corner. RStudio's help browser also has a search box on the upper right of its main toolbar to locate a help page, or the page can be opened with tab completion and the F1 key. Due to its web-technology roots, RStudio easily leverages R's HTML help system; pages appearing in the Help pane have active links.

After consulting the help page, we see that the format argument is needed. This specification is described elsewhere, in the help page for the strptime function. Clicking on the provided link opens that page, allowing us to figure out that the specification needed to make our function call is:

```
> x$datetime  <- paste(x$date, x$time)
> x$time <- as.POSIXct(x$datetime, format="%m/%d/%Y %H:%M:%S")
```

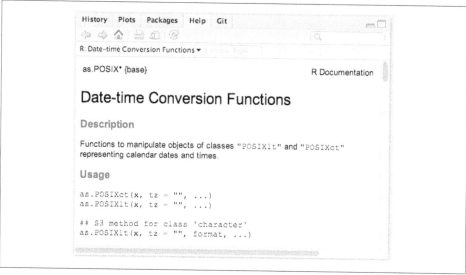

Figure 2-10. Help page for the POSIXct function

Data Cleaning

At this point we have a data frame, x, storing all the information we have about the colony of mole rats. However, the data set needs to be cleaned up, as there are some repeated observations. We do this on a per-rat basis. R has several ways to implement the split-apply-combine idiom, as it is one of the most useful patterns for R users. The plyr package is widely used, but for this task we use functions from base R. The split function can be used to divide the data by the grouping variable RFID, returning a list whose components are the records for the individual mole rats:

```
> l <- split(x, x$RFID)
```

The list, l, has a different component for each mole rat. We can check to see if any two rows for a mole rat are identical, using R's convenient duplicated method. In addition, we add a bit of time to to each time value, so that times recorded with the same second are distinguished. R has several different means to apply a function to pieces of an object. Below we use lapply to apply a function to each component of the list l, returning a new list l1 with the modified data:

```
> l1 <- lapply(l, function(x) {
+   trimmed <- x[duplicated(x),]
+   nr <- nrow(trimmed)
+   trimmed$time <- trimmed$time + seq_len(nr)/nr*(1/1000)
+   trimmed
+ })
```

The data is recorded by gate, but the actual item of interest is the bubble (chamber) the mole rat is in at a given time. This information allows us to consider how social an animal is by looking at the time shared with others. We need to deduce this information from the data.

We do so by assuming that if the mole rat is in bubble 5, say, and we record gate 5, then the mole rat moved to bubble 6. Or, if the recording was gate 4, then the mole rat moved to bubble 4. (There are 15 bubbles and 14 gates, so gate *i* is between bubbles *i* and *i+1*.) To create the bubble count, we assume the mole rat moves immediately to the bubble after crossing a gate. This ignores the possibility of the mole rat changing its mind and never actually going to the next bubble. We will use a for loop to do this computation.

Using the Code Editor to Write R Scripts

The actual command we need for this computation is a bit long to type in correctly at the command line. We will instead use a script file so we can freely edit our commands. RStudio makes it easy to evaluate lines from a script file in the console. In addition, with the aid of syntax highlighting and automatic code formatting, we can quickly identify common errors before evaluation.

The "open a new R Script file" action is proxied in several places: through the leftmost toolbar button in the application toolbar, through the File > New > R Script menu item, or through a keyboard shortcut (Ctrl+Shift+N). However invoked, once done, a new untitled file appears in the code-editor. In this new file we type in our commands, as shown in Figure 2-11. The figure also shows how the code editor component is used in many ways: to look at raw data sets, view rectangular data objects from the workspace, and edit R commands.

```
 1  l2  <- sapply(l1, function(x) {
 2    nr <- nrow(x)
 3    x$bubble <- numeric(nr)
 4    x$bubble[1] <- x$gate[1]  ## start somewhere
 5    for(i in 2:nr) {
 6      x$bubble[i] <- x$gate[i] +
 7        as.numeric(x$gate[i] >= x$bubble[i-1])
 8    }
 9    x
10  }, simplify=FALSE)
11
```

Figure 2-11. Using the source-code editor for multiline commands

With the commands typed in, we are ready to execute them. RStudio allows several variations on how to send the contents of a file to the console. In this case, we simply click on the Source toolbar button at the far right of the pane's toolbar to call source on the active document.

Using Add-On Packages

Each component of the l2 list contains records for a mole rat. The key variables are the times, stored as POSIXct values and bubble. It will be more convenient to use another of R's date-time classes to represent the data, as then many desirable methods will come along for free. Our data is an irregular time series, as time is marked by mole rat events, not regular intervals on the clock. The zoo package is designed for such data, as one needs only ordered observations for the time index.

To convert our data into zoo objects, we first need to load the package. RStudio makes working with packages easy through the Packages component, which for us appears in the lower-right pane. Loading or unloading a package is as simple as checking the package's accompanying checkbox to indicate the desired state (Figure 2-12), where a check indicates the package is loaded.

We had previously installed the zoo package, so it shows in the packages list. Were that not the case, we could have quickly installed the package from CRAN, along with any dependencies, using the dialog raised by clicking the leftmost Install Packages toolbar button in the pane's toolbar.

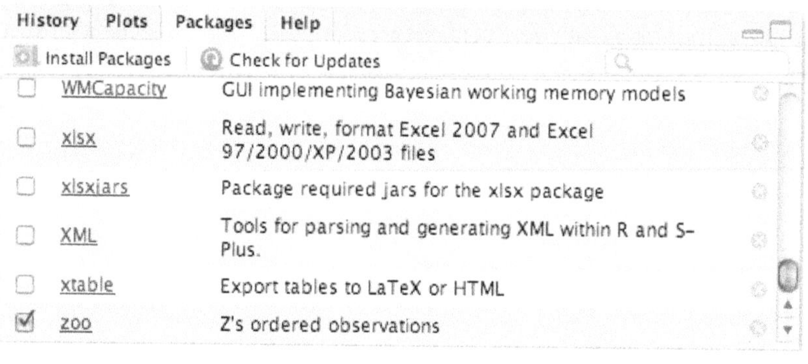

Figure 2-12. The Packages component allows you to select packages to load or unload and conveniently provides links to their documentation

To create a zoo object, we call its same-named constructor. The first argument is the data; the second the value to order by. We then merge the data into one zoo object. Here, we also use the na.locf function to carry the last bubble forward to replace an NA when the data is merged:

```
> l3  <- sapply(l2, function(x) zoo(x$bubble, x$time), simplify=FALSE)
> x  <- na.locf(do.call(merge, l3), na.rm=FALSE)
```

Graphics

One of the reasons we used a `zoo` object is its convenient `plot` method. We begin by making time series plots of the first five mole rats on the same graphic. We can't recall the specific arguments, so again let tab completion (Figure 2-13) lead us to the correct help page. In this case we type `plot`, and the function completion shows us the various `plot` methods available. Scrolling through, we find `plot.zoo`.

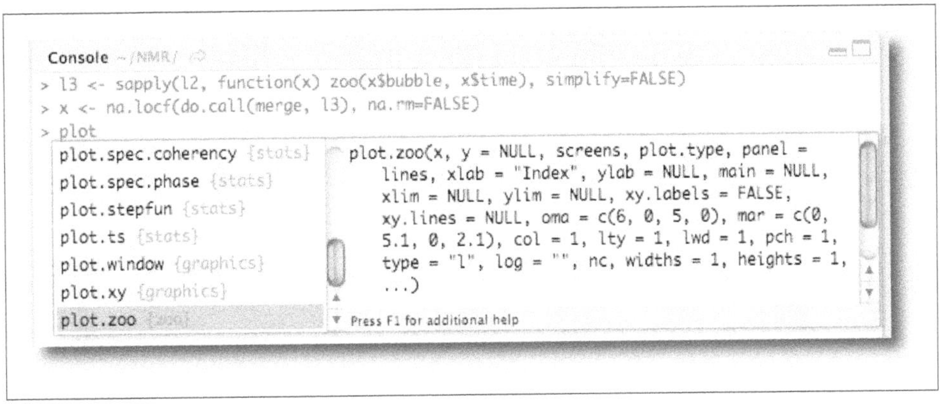

```
Console  ~/NMR/
> l3 <- sapply(l2, function(x) zoo(x$bubble, x$time), simplify=FALSE)
> x <- na.locf(do.call(merge, l3), na.rm=FALSE)
> plot

plot.spec.coherency {stats}       plot.zoo(x, y = NULL, screens, plot.type, panel =
plot.spec.phase {stats}               lines, xlab = "Index", ylab = NULL, main = NULL,
plot.stepfun {stats}                  xlim = NULL, ylim = NULL, xy.labels = FALSE,
plot.ts {stats}                       xy.lines = NULL, oma = c(6, 0, 5, 0), mar = c(0,
plot.window {graphics}                5.1, 0, 2.1), col = 1, lty = 1, lwd = 1, pch = 1,
plot.xy {graphics}                    type = "l", log = "", nc, widths = 1, heights = 1,
                                      ...)
plot.zoo {zoo}
                                  ▼ Press F1 for additional help
```

Figure 2-13. Using tab-key completion to find arguments to the plot method of zoo objects

In the figure we see the `plot.type` argument for this plot method but don't recall the values to specify the graphic we desire. As instructed, we press the F1 key to call up additional help in the help browser and read that `"single"` is the desired argument value.

After we issue the command:

```
> plot(x[, 1:5], plot.type="single")
```

the `Plots` component is raised, showing the plot.

Command History

Noting that the individual paths are hard to distinguish once they've crossed, we want to add colors to the graphic. The `col` argument is used for this. Rather than retype the previous command, we can edit it. RStudio keeps a record of previous commands. The up and down arrow shortcuts can be used to scroll through our command history. For more complicated usage, we can use the `History` component, which allows us to browse the past commands and reissue them. We use the up arrow for this case, then modify the `col` argument to a simple value of `1:5`, producing Figure 2-14.

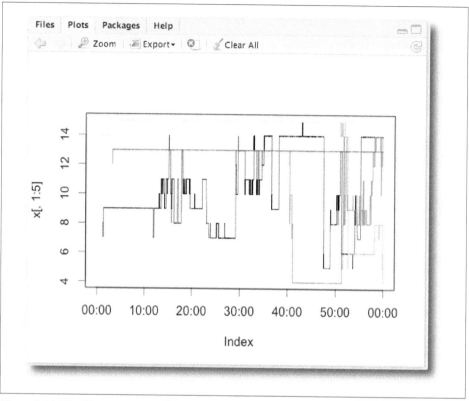

Figure 2-14. The Plots component showing a time-series plot of the first five cases

The plot is sized to fill the Plots pane, and can be on the small side. (Unlike most interactive R use, where the plot devices choose their size.) Often this is all that is needed, but in this particular case we wish it to be bigger. The Zoom toolbar button of the Plots component's toolbar will open the graph in a larger window.

All Finished, for Now

At this point, with the help of RStudio, we have completed the data preparation needed for subsequent analysis. We have a zoo object holding all the data (x) and a list of zoo objects (13) storing data for individual rats. In the process of this 30-minute analysis, we took advantage of most all of RStudio's key components: the Files browser, tab completion, the text editor, the Help browser, the rectangular data viewer, the Console, the Source code editor, the Packages browser, and the Plots viewer.

CHAPTER 3

The Console and Related Components

Interactive use of R is achieved through the command-line interface (CLI) provided by the Console component—this is where users issue commands for R to parse and then evaluate. RStudio provides a console that behaves pretty much like any other console R users have seen, such as the one provided by the RGui for Windows. This chapter describes command-line usage in RStudio, along with some of the components providing direct support for interactive usage.

Entering Commands

The simplest use of R involves typing one or more commands at the *prompt* (usually a > symbol) and then pressing the enter key. Commands can be combined on one line if separated by a semicolon and can extend over multiple lines. Once entered, the command is sent back to the R interpreter. If the commands are complete and there are no errors, R returns the output from the call. Usually, this output is displayed in the Console. The first command in Figure 3-1 shows how RStudio responds to the command to add 2 and 2. To distinguish parts of the text, the commands appear in one color and the output in another (by default). Some calls (e.g., assignment, graphic commands, function calls returned by invisible) return no printed output. In the RStudio console, the input and output may be perused by the user and copy-and-pasted, but may not be directly edited. (The History pane is used instead.)

When a command is not complete, R's parser will recognize this and allow the user to type onto the following line. In this case, the prompt turns to the *continuation prompt* (typically a +). Multiline commands can be entered in this manner. The last command in Figure 3-1 shows an example of the continuation prompt.

When a command containing an error is issued, RStudio returns the appropriate error message generated by R (Figure 3-2). For the experienced user, these error messages are usually very informative, but for beginning users they may be difficult to interpret.

```
Console ~/ ⇨                                    ▭ ☐
> 2 + 2
[1] 4
> 2 +
+ |
```

Figure 3-1. The first command shows printed output; the second one has a continuation prompt appear, as the command is syntactically valid but not complete during evaluation

Figure 3-2. The console displays error messages from the R interpreter

Many commands involve assignment to a variable. R has two commonly used options for assignment: = and ← (the latter is preferred by most longtime R users). The arrow assignment operator has a keyboard shortcut Alt+- (Option+- in Mac OS X), which makes it as easy to enter as the equals sign. Using the arrow is recommended—and as a bonus, extra space is inserted around the assignment operator for clarity.

The `Console` panel adds very few actions. As such, there is no toolbar. The current working directory (`getwd`) appears in the panel's title, along with an arrow icon to open the `Files` browser to display this directory's contents. The `Files` browser, by design, does not track the current working directory—but the title bar does, so this arrow can be a time saver.

The `width` option (`getOption("width")`) is consulted by many of R's functions in order to control the number of characters per line used in output. This value is conveniently updated when a user resizes the horizontal space allocated to the `Console`. Other options are also implemented to modify the various prompts, such as `prompt` and `continue`.

There are few instances where things can get too long:

Commands with lengthy output
   When the output of a command is too lengthy, it will be truncated. The option `max.print` will be consulted to make this determination. For server usage, one may wish to keep this small, as the data must be passed back from the server to be shown.

Commands with lengthy run times

Sometimes a command will take a long time to execute. This may be by design, but it also can be the result of an erroneous request. In the first case, one can inform the user of the state (e.g., `?txtProgressBar`). In the latter case, a user may wish to interrupt the evaluation. This is done using the Escape key or by clicking on the `Stop` icon that appears during a command's execution in the right side of the `Console` pane's title bar (Figure 3-3).

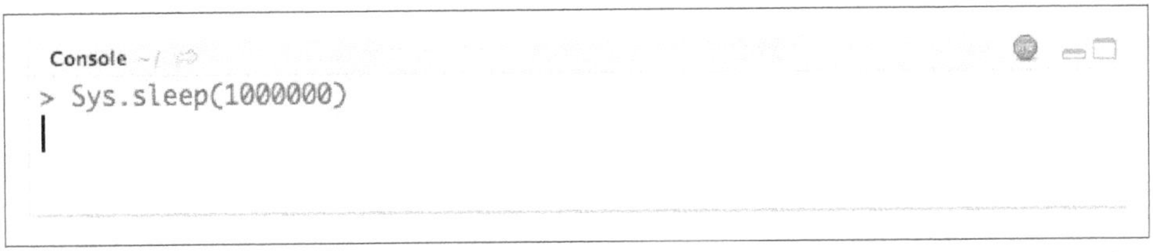

Figure 3-3. An icon to interrupt a command's evaluation appears during long-running commands

Automatic Insertion of Matching Pairs

In R, many characters come in pairs: parentheses, brackets, braces, and quotes ((, [, [[, ", and '). Failing to have a matching pair will often result in a parse error or an incomplete command, both annoyances. RStudio tries to circumvent this by automatically creating matching pairs when the first one is entered. That is, typing a left parenthesis adds a matching right one. Also, deleting one will can cause the other to be deleted if no text is entered in between.

While a useful convenience, this feature can be hard to get accustomed to, so it can be turned off. RStudio's Options dialog (Preferences in Mac OS X) provides a toggle button (Figure 3-4). Even if this feature is turned off, RStudio still provides assistance with matching pairs by highlighting the opening parenthesis, bracket, or brace when the cursor is positioned at the closing one.

R Script Files

The console is excellent for quick interactive commands but not as convenient for longer, multiline commands. For such tasks, being able to type the commands into a file to be executed as a block proves very useful. Not only is it easier to see the underlying logic of the commands and to find any errors, this style also allows one to easily archive commands for later reference. The RStudio `Source` editor (described more fully in "Source Code Editor" on page 61) can be used for writing scripts and executing blocks of code from them.

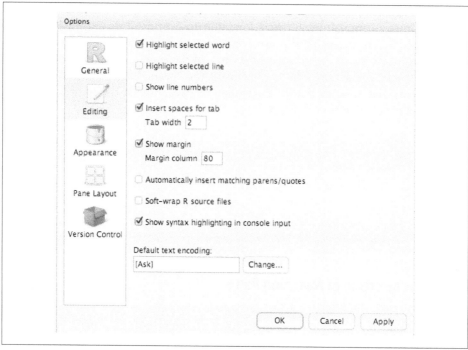

Figure 3-4. The Options dialog has the ability to turn off automatic matching of paired values

A new R script file can be opened in the code editor using the leftmost toolbar button on the application toolbar or from the `File > New > R Script` menu item. Into this file a series of commands may be typed. There are different actions available that execute these commands in part or in total:

Run line or selection
Run the current line or selection. Commands that are run are added to the history stack ("Command History" on page 33).

Run all lines
Run all the lines in the buffer.

Run from beginning to line or run from line to end
Run lines above or below the current line including current.

Run function
Have RStudio look for the function enclosing the cursor and run that.

Rerun previous region
This allows one to edit a region and rerun its contents without needing to reselect it.

Source (or Source with echo)
Call source on the file ("source with echo" will echo back the commands). Sourced commands do not add to the history stack.

These actions are invoked via the menu bar, keyboard shortcut, or toolbar button. All appear under the Edit menu item and have their corresponding keyboard shortcut shown (Table 3-2). The toolbar buttons for the editor allow one to run the line or selection quickly, rerun the previous region, or source the buffer into R.

Command-Line Conveniences

Working with a command line has a long history. Despite the popularity of GUIs, command lines still have many aficionados, as they are more expressive—and, once some conveniences are learned—usually much faster to use. For reproducible research they are great, as they can record the exact commands used. There are drawbacks, though. Typing can be a chore, proper command syntax is essential, and the user needs to have intimate knowledge of the function and its arguments. All of these can be huge obstacles to newcomers to R. Over time, these drawbacks of command-line usage have been lessened through techniques such as tab completion, keyboard shortcuts, and history stacks.

We discuss RStudio's implementation of these next. Becoming well-versed in these features can help you turn the command line from a distant stranger into a welcome friend.

Tab Completion

Working at the command line requires users to remember function names and the names of their arguments. To save keystrokes, many R users rely on tab completion to complete partially typed commands. The basic idea of tab completion is that when the user has a partially completed command and the Tab key is pressed, the command will be completed if there is only one candidate for completion. If there is more than one, a menu of candidates is given to choose from. The implementation of this feature varies across the different R interfaces, although most implement it—none, perhaps, as intuitively as RStudio. Here the menu provided for candidate selection is a context-sensitive completion dialog raised (when needed) by pressing the Tab key and dismissed by making a selection or by pressing either the Backspace or Escape key.

The completion dialog (see Figure 3-5) has a left pane with options that can be scrolled through, and usually a right pane providing details on the selection (if available). This short description is great for jogging memories as to what the value effects. The corresponding help page that contains this information can be opened by pressing the F1 key.

A candidate value for completion may be selected with a mouse, but it is typically more convenient to use the keyboard. Press the up or down arrow to scroll through the list and use the Enter key (or Tab key again) to select the currently highlighted value for insertion. Typing a new character will narrow the list of candidates.

The completion window depends on the context of the cursor when the Tab key is pressed. Here are some scenarios:

Completion of object and function names

When an object or function name is partially typed, the completion candidates will be objects on the user's search path whose case-sensitive name begins with the value. Objects may be in the global workspace of the user or available objects from the loaded packages (functions, variables, and data sets). In the latter case, the package name appears next to the value and, when possible, a summary of the object from its help page (Figure 3-5).

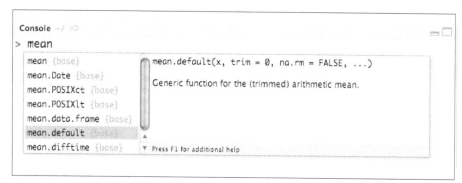

Figure 3-5. Completion for an object in the workspace shows the full name, its package (when applicable), and a short description if available

Listing of function arguments

If the cursor is inside the matched pair of parentheses enclosing a function's arguments and the Tab key is pressed, the arguments will populate the completion candidates (Figure 3-6). The arguments appear with an = appended to their name, to distinguish them from objects.

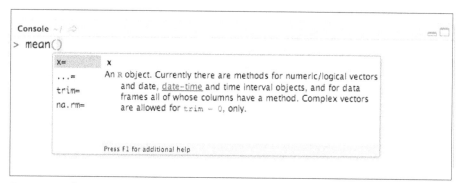

Figure 3-6. The completion window for function arguments shows information from the help page

Completion within a function's argument list

Within a populated argument list, the completion code provides arguments and objects, as both may be desired (Figure 3-7). R can use named arguments or positional arguments where only the object is specified.

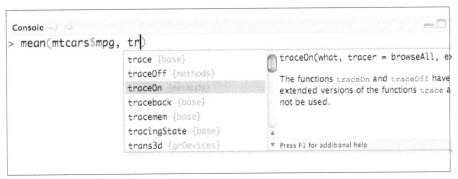

Figure 3-7. Completion with a function from a partial description shows that candidates include arguments and objects

Completion within strings

Within quotes, the completion code will offer a list of files and subdirectories to choose from (Figure 3-8). By default, this will list files and directories in the working directory, but if any part of a path is given (absolute or using the "tilde" expansion) then files and directories relative to that are presented.

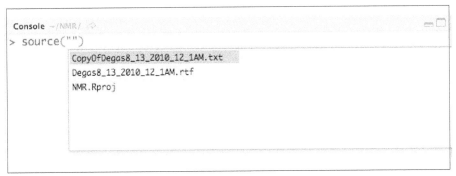

Figure 3-8. A Tab-key completion of strings uses files in the current directory for candidates

The selection of completion candidates is eventually delegated to a framework provided by R's `utils` package and documented under `rcompgen`. That help page has much more detail on how the completion candidates are figured out. For example, completion can be done after the extractors `$` (for lists and environments) and `@` (for S4 objects). In this case, the completion window has no details pane. Additionally, completion can be carried out inside namespaces, even when not exported (using `:::`).

There are a few limitations of the completion mechanism. Completion of function arguments can be difficult for generic functions, as the argument list may depend on the specified arguments and these are not evaluated; and the token for completion is found by considering the current line, so it doesn't work well with multiline commands.

Keyboard Shortcuts

Keyboard shortcuts allow the user to quickly invoke common actions by pressing the appropriate keyboard combination. For example, many people have their fingers trained for the copy and paste keyboard shortcuts, as using them can be more convenient than using a mouse to initiate these actions. RStudio has numerous keyboard shortcuts. In keeping with standard GUI design, many of these appear alongside the menu item associated with the action. Here, we discuss those shortcuts that are implemented for the console and its integration with the source-code editor.

Keyboard shortcuts are usually operating-system dependent, and RStudio's are no exception (though, they are not locale specific). Additionally, keybindings may also be editor-dependent. In particular, the well-established `vi` and `Emacs` keybindings are hardwired into many users' fingers. The RStudio keybindings are a mix of OS-consistent bindings (e.g., copy and paste in Windows is Ctrl+C and Ctrl+V, and in Mac OS X, Cmd+C and Cmd+V) and Emacs-specific (e.g., Ctrl+K will kill all the text to the right of the cursor [including the end-of-line character] and Ctrl+Y will yank it back [paste it in]). Although `vi` users may feel left out, adding in the Emacs bindings surely makes many longtime R users happy—it is hard to retrain one's fingers! Similar shortcuts have been present for a long time in R's console through the `readline` library.

In Table 1-2, we listed shortcuts for navigation between components. Here in Table 3-1, we describe shortcuts for working at the console, and in Table 3-2 list the available shortcuts for sending commands from the source-code editor to the console. General editing shortcuts for the console and source editor are listed later in Table 5-1.

 In RStudio, keybindings are currently not customizable. Keeping consistency across platforms, the web interface, and the *Qt* desktop is difficult. Keyboard shortcuts do get updated on occasion. The current list is found under the menu item `Help > Keyboard Shortcuts`.

Table 3-1. Console-specific keyboard shortcuts

Description	Windows and Linux	Mac
Move cursor to console	Ctrl+2	Ctrl+2
Clear console	Ctrl+L	Command+L
Move cursor to beginning of line	Home	Command+Left
Move cursor to end of line	End	Command+Right
Navigate command history	Up/Down	Up/Down
Pop-up command history	Ctrl+Up	Command+Up
Interrupt currently executing command	Esc	Esc
Change working directory	Ctrl+Shift+K	Ctrl+Shift+K

Table 3-2. Keyboard shortcuts for running commands in the Source editor

Description	Windows and Linux	Mac
Run current line/selection	Ctrl+Enter	Command+Enter
Run current document	Ctrl+Shift+R	Command+Shift+R
Run from document beginning to current line	Ctrl+Shift+B	Command+Shift+B
Run from current line to document end	Ctrl+Shift+E	Command+Shift+E
Run the current function definition	Ctrl+Shift+F	Command+Shift+F
Rerun previous region	Ctrl+Shift+P	Command+Shift+P
Source a file	Ctrl+Shift+0	Command+Shift+0
Source the current document	Ctrl+Shift+S	Command+Shift+S

Command History

Interactive usage often involves repeating a past command or parts of a command. Perhaps one wishes to change an argument's value, or perhaps there was a minor error. Retyping an entire command to make a minor change is tedious at best. A common instinct is to insert the cursor at the error and edit the previously issued command, but this is not typically supported by console usage. One might then be tempted to copy and paste the command to the prompt and proceed to edit. Though this works, the history mechanism speeds up this process.

RStudio keeps a stack of past commands and allows one to scroll through them easily. This can be done using the up and down arrow keys. As the arrows are pressed, the previous commands are copied to the prompt, allowing them to be edited. The list of commands can be scrolled through quickly.

To see more than one previous command at a time, the Ctrl+Up keyboard shortcut can be typed, and a history window, similar to that for tab completion, will pop up (Figure 3-9).

```
Console  ~/Downloads/
[ 2 1  TRUE   TRUE   TRUE
[   AND(d)                                        ▲
>   AND(d)
    ANY(x > 0)
1   AND(x > 0)
2   AND(as.data.frame(x > 0))
3   AND(x > 0)
>
[   AND(as.data.frame(x > 0))
>   AND = function(x) UseMethod("AND")
>   AND.default = function(x) Reduce("&", x)
>   AND.matrix = function(x) AND(as.data.frame(x))   ))
>   AND(x > 0)
[1,
> AN
```

Figure 3-9. History pop up opened by Ctrl+Up or, as in this case, Ctrl+R. The latter narrows the history candidates by searching for previous command completions

Searching the history stack

Searching (as opposed to scrolling) through the past history (Ctrl+R on many R consoles) is better for lengthy sessions. RStudio implements searching its own way. Calling Ctrl+Up when there is text already typed at the prompt will narrow the list shown in the history pop up to just commands beginning with that text. One can use the arrow keys or mouse to select a value. Alternatively, one can continue typing, which causes the pop up to close and reopen with a narrowed list.

History Browser

In addition to the command-line interaction with a user's history, RStudio also provides a History browser (Figure 3-10), allowing the user to scroll through past commands or use a search box. The past commands are organized in time order, with timestamps added for extended sessions. By default, this component resides in a tab on the upper right, and may be raised by clicking on the tab or using the shortcut Ctrl+4.

The basic usage involves double-clicking a line, which sends it to the console to be edited or reissued (the focus shifts to the console, so just pressing the Enter key will re-execute the command). Other uses involve first marking a selection. A single click selects the line, and this selection can be extended by holding the Shift key and using the up and down arrows. Other selection modifications are also possible. The component's toolbar has three buttons: one sends the selection to the console, one appends the selection to a file in the source-code editor (opening one if need be), and one removes the selection from the history list (the page icon with the red "x"). If a multiline selection is sent to the console, no continuation prompt is inserted, allowing one to edit any of the lines.

The toolbar also has icons to save the history to a file, read the history in from a file, and clear the history in its entirety.

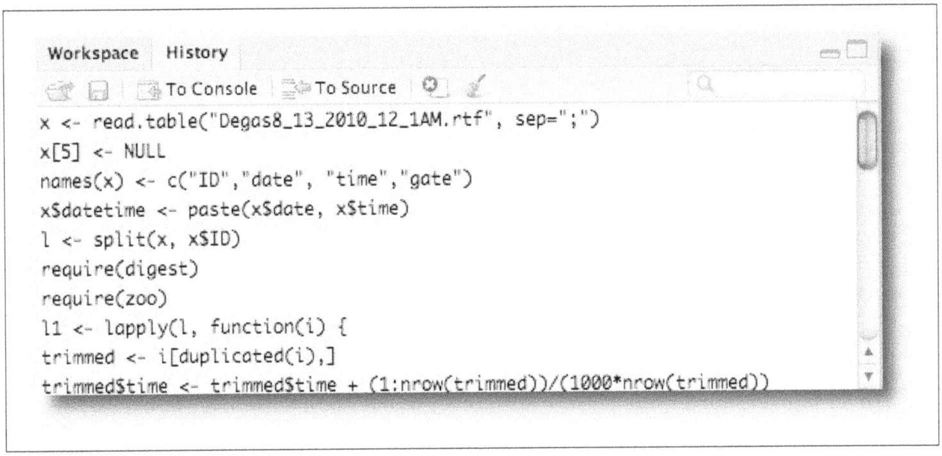

```
Workspace   History

         To Console      To Source

x <- read.table("Degas8_13_2010_12_1AM.rtf", sep=";")
x[5] <- NULL
names(x) <- c("ID","date", "time","gate")
x$datetime <- paste(x$date, x$time)
l <- split(x, x$ID)
require(digest)
require(zoo)
ll <- lapply(l, function(i) {
trimmed <- i[duplicated(i),]
trimmed$time <- trimmed$time + (1:nrow(trimmed))/(1000*nrow(trimmed))
```

Figure 3-10. The history component shows the session history, which allows commands to be recycled

The General panel of the options dialog has a couple of entries related to the history-recording mechanism: one to modify how the history is saved and one to toggle the option to remove duplicate commands.

Workspace Browser

When an R user assigns a value to a variable, the assignment is held in an *environment*, R's way of organizing its objects. Environments are nested, and this nesting is traversed to locate variable assignments. The user's global workspace (.GlobalEnv) is the top-level environment where names are bound during interactive use (Figure 3-11). This workspace is typically persistent—that is, a user is prompted to save it when quitting an R session, and it is loaded on startup or when a new project is selected (see "Which Workspace?" on page 7). Over time, there can be many variables, and remembering what they are can become nearly impossible. R has some functions to list the variables in an environment (primarily ls), but RStudio makes this much easier through its Workspace browser.

The Workspace browser appears by default as a tabbed pane in the upper-right of the GUI. The browser lists the objects in the global workspace, organized by type of value: Data, Values, Functions.

The global workspace is not the only environment that R uses. Indeed, it is just one of many. For example, without extra work, within a function assignment occurs in the function's environment and disappears when the function exits. Such assignments do not appear in the Work space browser.

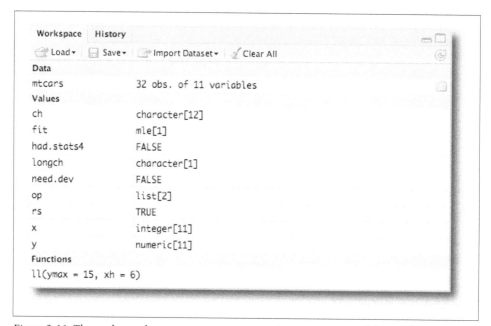

Figure 3-11. The workspace browser component summarizes objects in the global workspace; objects can be viewed or edited

Editing and Viewing Objects

Clicking on a value will initiate an action to edit or view the object. Currently, rectangular objects, such as data frames and matrices, are not editable. For these, RStudio provides an implementation for View (really dataentry).

For other objects, how the value gets edited depends on the type of object and its length.

For some atomic objects with length 1, the editing occurs within the Workspace browser (Figure 3-12). Clicking on the object highlights its value, which can then be edited using the browser as a property editor. The input expression is not evaluated and need not be of the same class.

More typically, clicking on an object invokes an editor in a pop-up window. In Figure 3-13, we see the editor appearing after clicking on the ch variable, a character vector of length 12.

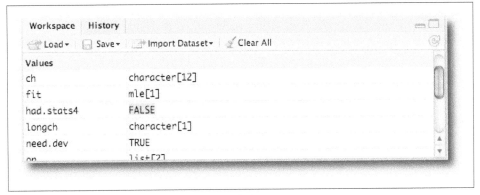

Figure 3-12. Atomic objects of length 1 are edited inline

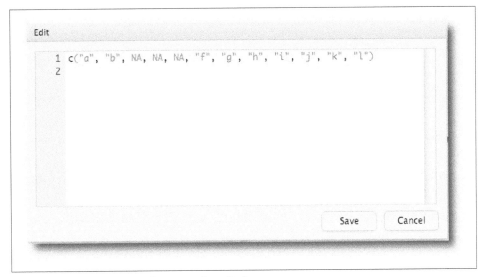

Figure 3-13. Simple pop-up editor is used to edit data vectors

One can edit and save, or simply cancel. Similarly, one can edit functions through the same editor.

Editing an object involves first deparsing the object into a file and then calling the editor on that file. When editing is finished, the text is parsed and, if there is no error, this value is assigned (see ?edit for details). Editing of functions preserves the function environment. Editing of some objects—for instance, S4 objects—is not possible.

For data frames and matrices, there is a data viewer. Clicking on such an object will open a view of the data in the code-editor pane similar to Figure 3-14. At the time of this writing, the view is limited to 100 columns and 1,000 lines. This view is a snapshot and is not updated if the underlying object changes. However, reclicking the object in the `Workspace` browser will refresh the view.

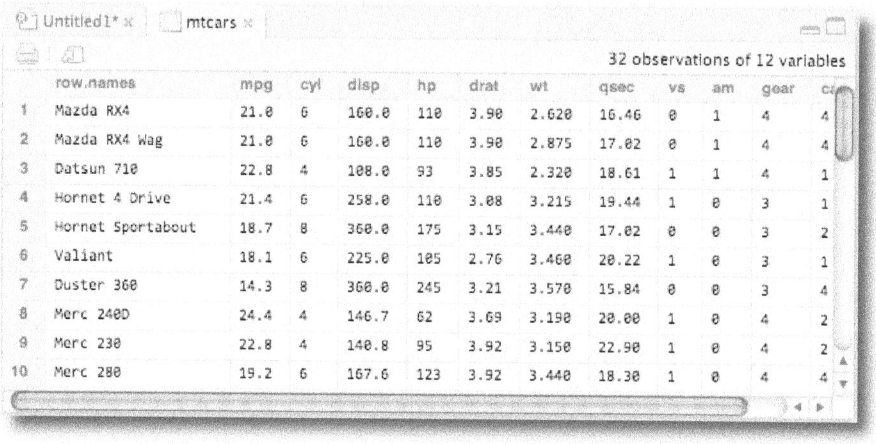

	row.names	mpg	cyl	disp	hp	drat	wt	qsec	vs	am	gear	ca
1	Mazda RX4	21.0	6	160.0	110	3.90	2.620	16.46	0	1	4	4
2	Mazda RX4 Wag	21.0	6	160.0	110	3.90	2.875	17.02	0	1	4	4
3	Datsun 710	22.8	4	108.0	93	3.85	2.320	18.61	1	1	4	1
4	Hornet 4 Drive	21.4	6	258.0	110	3.08	3.215	19.44	1	0	3	1
5	Hornet Sportabout	18.7	8	360.0	175	3.15	3.440	17.02	0	0	3	2
6	Valiant	18.1	6	225.0	105	2.76	3.460	20.22	1	0	3	1
7	Duster 360	14.3	8	360.0	245	3.21	3.570	15.84	0	0	3	4
8	Merc 240D	24.4	4	146.7	62	3.69	3.190	20.00	1	0	4	2
9	Merc 230	22.8	4	140.8	95	3.92	3.150	22.90	1	0	4	2
10	Merc 280	19.2	6	167.6	123	3.92	3.440	18.30	1	0	4	4

Figure 3-14. The data-frame viewer provided by RStudio is rendered in the Source-editor pane

The `Workspace` browser has a few other features available through its toolbar for manipulating the workspace:

- Previously saved workspaces (or the default one) can be loaded through a dialog invoked by the `Load` toolbar button.
- The current workspace can be saved either as the default workspace (`.RData` file) or to an alternate file.
- The entire workspace can be cleared through the `Clear All` toolbar button. To delete single items, one can use the `rm` function through the console.

Importing Data Sets

Importing data into an R session can be done in numerous ways, as there are many different data formats. The *R Data Import/Export* manual provides details for common cases. For properly formatted text files, RStudio provides the `Import Dataset` toolbar button to open a dialog to initiate the process. You select where the file resides (locally, or as a web resource), then a dialog opens to select the file. Once a file is specified (and possibly downloaded/uploaded), a dialog appears that allows you to customize how the data will be imported. Figure 3-15 shows the defaults for reading in the `mtcars` data when first written out as a `csv` file.

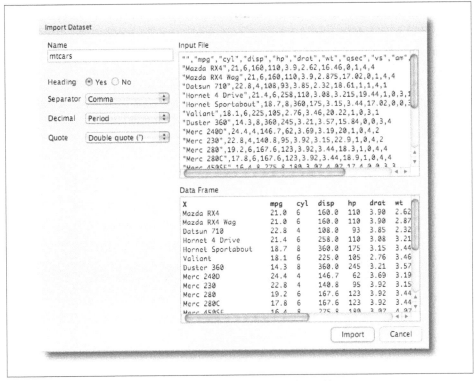

Figure 3-15. Dialog for importing a data set from a formatted text file

The dialog has the more commonly used arguments for a call to `read.table`, but it is missing a few, such as `comment.char`.

> For server usage, one can upload arbitrary files into the working directory through the `Files` browser (see "The File Browser" on page 69).

The Help Page Viewer

As mentioned, R is enhanced by external code organized into packages. Packages are a structured means for the functions and objects that extend R. Part of this organization extends to documentation. R has a few ways of documenting itself in a package. For packages on CRAN, compliance is checked automatically. Each exported function should be documented in a help page. This page typically contains a description of the function, a description of its arguments, additional information potentially of use to the user, and, optionally, some example code. Multiple functions may share the same documentation file. In addition to examples for a function, a package may contain demos to illustrate key functionality and *vignettes* (longer documents describing the package and what it provides).

R has its own format, *Rd* format, for marking up its help pages. This format is well described in *Writing R Extensions*, one of the manuals that accompanies R. As the `Rd` format is structured, functions (in the `tools` package) have been written to convert the text to HTML format. R comes with a local web server to display these pages. RStudio can show them as well, and does so in its `Help` browser. By default, this component (Figure 3-16) appears in the pane in the lower-right corner.

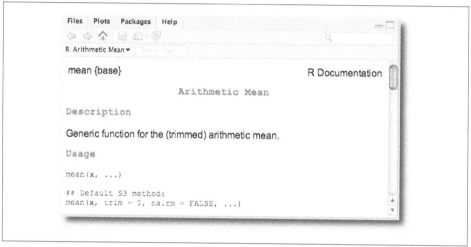

Figure 3-16. The Help browser component shows R's help pages

Help pages are invoked by the `help` function, although the easy-to-type shortcut ? is typically used. For example, executing `?mean` will open the help page for the `mean` function from the `base` package (Figure 3-16).

An advantage of HTML rendering of help pages is that the provided links are active. For example, in the `mean` help page, the help page author provides links (Figure 3-17) to `weighted.mean` (for computing a mean with weights), `mean.POSIXct` (an `S3` method for computing the mean of time data), and `colMeans`.

The add-on `helpr` package for R enhances the appearance of the help pages by applying attractive CSS styling, adding a comment feature, and providing the ability to execute the examples directly from the `Help` browser.

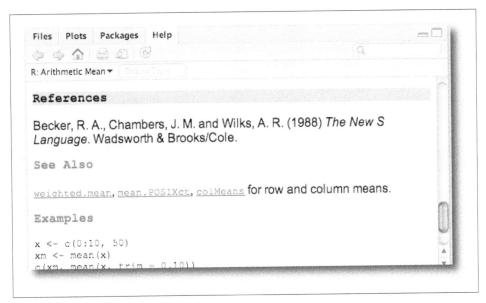

Figure 3-17. Help pages have active links

The ? shortcut is the most basic functionality for help. In the Packages pane, the installed packages appear as a link. Clicking such a link opens a description page for the package (as would a command like help(package="package_name")). This description page gives links to the documented functions, and in addition (if applicable) provides access to the DESCRIPTION file, the NEWS file, a list of demos, and any package vignettes.

The ?? shortcut allows quicker access to R's help.search function. This allows for searching the help system's documentation for a match to the specific pattern, searching within the alias, title, and concept entries. (The help.search function allows a more refined search.) As of R 2.14.0, the results are returned in a search results page in the Help browser with links to the different matches.

There are two different search boxes provided by the Help browser. The box in the upper-right corner of the main toolbar (Figure 3-18) lists the available help topics matching the beginning of the typed expression, using an auto-completion feature. This serves a similar, but more convenient, role as the apropos function, which can be used to search for workspace objects matching a pattern. The lower search box in the secondary toolbar is used to search through the contents of the displayed help page.

Searching for text in RStudio is complicated by the presence of the many different panels. Basic search happens through the source-code editor; other searches are facilitated by panel-specific search boxes.

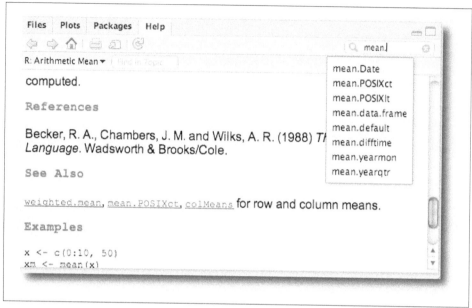

Figure 3-18. The upper search box of the Help browser displays possible matches

In addition to the search box, the Help browser's main toolbar provides other functionality:

- The arrows are used to scroll through the history of one's help-page usage. This history also appears as the values of a pop-up combobox when a help page is shown.

- Clicking the "home" toolbar button opens a page providing, among other items, links to the manuals that accompany R.

- The show in new window toolbar button will open the page in a web browser.

Searching online resources

R is widely discussed on internet forums and news groups. The RSite Search command is used to search for key words or phrases from various sources of help that exist online and in packages, through *http://search.r-project.org*. This command opens a browser window containing the results. The sos package provides an alternative interface.

Other useful places to find information about R or RStudio are the R mailing lists, the Stack Overflow thread for R at *http://stackover-flow.com/questions/tagged/r*, and the RStudio support forum at *http://support.rstudio.org*.

Graphics in RStudio

R, as a computing environment, is well known for its abilities to produce publication-quality graphics. Indeed, R graphics are often seen on the pages of *The New York Times*. To achieve this quality, the graphics engines in R have many levels of customization. Over the years, R has developed several different engines for producing graphics:

- The base graphics system offers easy-to-use statistics-oriented graphs and underlying low-level functions to allow users to design their own.

- The `lattice` package implements *Trellis* Graphics (an implementation of ideas in *Visualizing Data*, by William S. Cleveland [Hobart Press]) for `S` and `S-Plus`. Lattice graphics are very well suited for displaying multivariate data. Many standard statistical plots are easy to make, but an underlying flexibility allows users to create their own graphics.

- The `ggplot2` package provides a relatively recent third approach. This is an implementation by H. Wickham of ideas in *The Grammar of Graphics* by L. Wilkinson, et al. (Springer). It advertises that it combines the advantages of base and lattice graphics—in addition, it produces very attractive graphics. Again, one can quickly generate stock graphs, but there is much flexibility to build up a graph step by step.

All three of these systems rely on R's underlying graphics framework. R uses a paper-and-pen approach to graphics. A graphic device (the paper) is created or cleared, and the graphic commands then write (with pen) onto this paper in steps. The point of this analogy is that one can't erase the paper. (The `cranvas` package will provide an alternative to this, but that is a different topic.) As such, it is important to plan a graphic prior to creating it—for example, computing the size of the coordinate space that will be needed. (Don't worry, this is usually done for you by the calling function.) The device (or piece of paper) is quite flexible in general. It can be an interactive device or a device that writes to a file in a certain format, such as *pdf*, *png*, or *svg*.

Don't be turned off by the apparent complexity hinted at above. Although both the `lattice` and `ggplot2` packages are documented in book-length formats, this only reflects their underlying flexibility. All three graphics approaches provide enough higher-level functions that make the standard graphics of statistics as simple as remembering the function name and specifying the data appropriately.

The Plots Browser

RStudio provides its own device for the display of graphics, `RStudioGD`. By default, the device's output is rendered in the `Plots` browser. Although the graphics are secretly image files, the `RStudioGD` device also allows for interactivity. In Figure 3-19 we see a graph from one of the examples of `stat_contour` from `ggplot2` displayed in the browser.

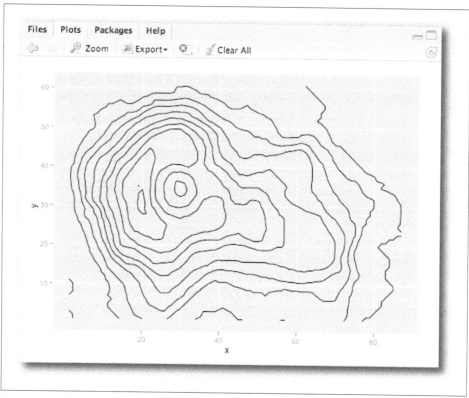

Figure 3-19. Plots browser showing a graphic produced by R

The image is initially sized to fit the space allocated to the browser. If the browser is resized, the image will be regenerated to match the new size. This happens in the background, though there is a button to refresh the current plot on the component's toolbar. If one desires an even larger view, the zoom toolbar button will open the graphic in a much larger Plot Zoom pop-up window. The zoom window is not an interactive device but a snapshot of the current graphic.

One benefit of how the device works is that a new graphic is produced each time (unlike many R devices, which essentially have an erase feature). This makes it easy for the component to keep a list of the graphics that are produced. One can scroll through old graphics using the left and right arrows located on the toolbar.

The currently viewed graphic can be exported as an image or *.pdf* file. RStudio provides a few dialogs to control this. In Figure 3-20, we see that the save-plot dialog allows one to easily specify the file type, directory, and file name of the image, as well as adjust the size of the image in pixels. The size can be adjusted by entering a value, or by dynamically adjusting the size with the grab handle in the lower right.

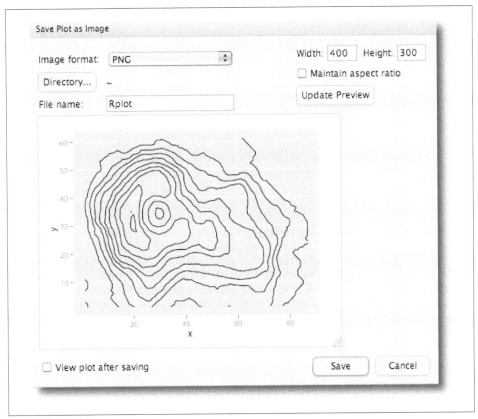

Figure 3-20. Export dialog for producing a graphic file for a plot

In addition, there are toolbar buttons to remove the current plot and to clear all the plots.

Interactivity

R allows for interaction with a graphic through the `locator` function, which returns the position of the point (in the "user coordinate system") where the (first) mouse button is pressed; and the `identify` function, which returns the index of the point nearest to where the (first) mouse button is pressed. Both functions are implemented for the RStudioGD device.

When the functions are called, the `Plots` browser is raised (if it wasn't already). The two functions are blocking, in that no input into the console is available until after the selection of coordinates is done. The console shows its stop icon, and the graphic device displays a message (Figure 3-21) that the locator is active, and instructs the user to press the Finish button. (For `locator`, one specifies ahead of time the number of points to identify, so the block will terminate if that occurs as well.)

Figure 3-21. When identify or locator is blocking input, the graphic window displays an alert

Some devices for R implement more complicated events, through get GraphicsEvent, but this is not currently the case for the RStudio device.

The manipulate Package for RStudio

Through the tcltk package (and others), an R programmer can create graphics that can have associated GUI controls to manipulate the display. Through the manipulate package, RStudio users can too. This package is provided with RStudio and delivers a set of simple-to-define controls that provide values to an expression used for plotting. These controls include a button, a slider, a picker, and a checkbox.

The basic usage is:

- One defines an expression that, when evaluated, produces the desired plot.
- This expression includes parameters labeled with the names given to the controls.
- When a control is updated, the expression is reevaluated and the graphic updated.

To illustrate, Figure 3-22 shows the code that implements the tkdensity demo from the tcltk package (there are 103 lines in the original, but just 16 here).

When the commands are executed, RStudio produces a plot based on the initial values of the control and also pops up a window with the controls as shown in Figure 3-23). Manipulating these controls will update the graphic (but not add to the history of graphics). The control frame's visibility is toggled through the double arrow icon in the control bar and the gear icon in the plot window.

This example shows three control types. A slider appears with both its own label, another label indicating the value, and a slider widget to adjust that value. The pickers are rendered using comboboxes, and the checkbox is displayed with its accompanying label.

```
tkdensity-in-manipulate.R ×
         Source on Save   🔍 ✎ ▾                              ↳Run  ⬐  Source ▾
require(manipulate)
dens <- list("Normal"=rnorm, "Exponential"=rexp)

manipulate({
  ## plot expression
  y <- dens[[distribution]](n)
  plot(density(y, bw=bw, kernel=kernel))
  if(addPoints)
    points(y, rep(0,l ength(y)))
},
            ## define controls
            n =slider(5, 100, initial=10),
            distribution=picker("Normal","Exponential"),
            kernel = picker("gaussian", "epanechnikov", "rectangular",
                            "triangular", "cosine"),
            bw = slider(.05,2, initial=1),
            addPoints=checkbox(TRUE, "Add points")
            )|

18:13   ☰ (Top Level) ≑                                      R Script ≑
```

Figure 3-22. *Example R code for using the manipulate package for interactive graphics*

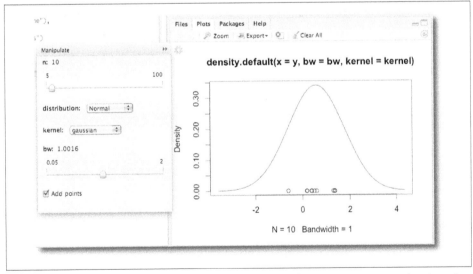

Figure 3-23. *The manipulate function creates a control panel for setting parameter values in a plot*

External Programs (Desktop Version)

R has several packages that provide interfaces to external programs and systems. For the desktop version of RStudio, in many cases one can call these to extend the interface (though such interactions can be temperamental.) For example, the tcltk package interfaces R with the Tk libraries for creating graphical user interfaces. The widely used Rcmdr package uses this package to provide a set of graphical interfaces to numerous R functions. The use of the tcltk package, as well as others such as RGtk2 and rJava, can be a little inconsistent under RStudio—though in many setups, they will work.

In addition, the desktop user can take advantage of R's internal help server. The package googleVis uses this to display Google's visualization tools in a browser. The Rook package provides an API for R users to write web applications that take advantage of this same server.

CHAPTER 4

Case Study: Creating a Package

Before describing more systematically the components that RStudio provides for development work in R (most importantly the source-code editor), we will pick up where we left off on our case study of analyzing the group behavior and individual movements of a colony of naked mole rats. Here, our goal is to illustrate one way to do package development with RStudio.

Imagine after a short time using RStudio for interactive use, that we are pretty happy using the command line for short commands, but have learned to really enjoy writing scripts in the Code editor. Even 2- or 3-line commands are much easier to debug when done in the editor. The directness of typing at the command line isn't lost, as our fingers are now trained to hit Ctrl+Enter to send the current line or selection to the R interpreter —or even Ctrl+Shift+Enter to send the entire buffer (Command, not Ctrl, for Mac users). We never need to leave the keyboard unless we choose to.

Along the way, we have been able to create a large script file that we now want to share with a colleague.

How do we do this? There are many ways. We could just send along the entire script, or with just a bit more extra work, we could share our work through a version control system. In some cases, this approach might be the best thing to do, as then our colleague can do exactly what we have been doing. However, there are many situations where this isn't so great. For example, perhaps this colleague doesn't know R too well and she just wants to have some functions to use. Plus, she may want to have some documentation on how to actually use the functions. Besides, we might want to share our work much more widely. At times like this, R users start to think about *packages*.

Packages are how R users extend R in a structured, reusable way. CRAN houses over 3,000 of them, and many more are scattered widely throughout the internet at R-specific repositories like those hosted by the Bioconductor project or on r-forge. Packages also appear on code-hosting sites such as *http://github.com* or *http://code.google.com*. However, we don't need to get packages from a website. We can start by creating our own *local* packages to share with colleagues. Let's see how, taking advantage of the features of the code-editor component of RStudio.

Creating Functions from Script Files

Currently, our script is one long set of commands that processes the data files and then makes a plot. We first want to turn some of the commands into *functions*. Functions make code reuse much more feasible. A basic pattern in R is to write functions for simple small tasks and then chain these tasks together using *function composition*. This is similar to the composition concept from mathematics, where we take the output from one function and use this as the input for another.

RStudio's integrated Source code editor—where we wrote our script—makes working with functions quite easy. We'll illustrate some of the features here.

For our task, we have a script that does four things to process the data:

1. It reads in the data and does some data cleaning.
2. It creates zoo objects for each mole rat.
3. It merges these into one large zoo object.
4. It makes a plot.

This naturally lends itself to four functions. Keeping our functions small and focused on a single task makes them easier to test and debug. It can also help later on in the development of a package, when we may think about combining similar tasks into more general functions, although we won't see that here.

RStudio provides a convenient action for turning a series of commands into a function. The magic wand toolbar button in the code editor has the Extract Function action. We simply highlight the text we want and then wave the magic wand—tada! In Figures 4-1 and 4-2, we illustrate the changes introduced by the magic wand. Our first function will be the one that reads the data into a data frame where the time column is using one of R's date classes.

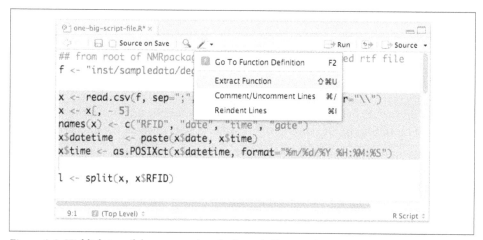

Figure 4-1. Highlighting of the commands to be "wanded" into a function

```
one-big-script-file.R* ×
    Source on Save                                    Run      Source
  1  f <- "~/NMR/CopyOfDegas8_13_2010_12_1AM.txt"
  2
  3  readNMRData <- function (f) {
  4    x <- read.csv(f, sep=";", header=FALSE, comment.char="\\")
  5
  6    x <- x[, - 5]
  7    names(x) <- c("RFID", "date", "time", "gate")
  8
  9    x$datetime  <- paste(x$date, x$time)
 10    x$time <- as.POSIXct(x$datetime, format="%m/%d/%Y %H:%M:%S")
 11
 12    x
 13  }
 14
 15
3:27    readNMRData                                            R Script
```

Figure 4-2. A function generated by the magic wand, where the argument and return value was added by hand

The magic wand does most of the work, but not all in this case, as the text can't adequately be parsed. In R, functions have arguments, a body of commands, a return value, and optionally are assigned to a name. We specify the name in the extract-function dialog, but for this instance added the function argument "f" and the return value "x" after the extraction.

We don't try to automate the process of converting the *rtf* file into a *txt* file, as that isn't so easy. We will put together the commands to process the data frame and create a list of zoo objects (one for each mole rat) and the commands to create a multivariate zoo object. This will be done with the magic wand in a similar manner as above.

A Package Skeleton

Packages must have a special structure, detailed in the *Writing R Extensions* manual that accompanies a standard R installation. We can consult that for detailed reference, but for now all we need to know is that the function package.skeleton will set up this structure for us. (The ProjectTemplate package can be used to provide even more detail to this process.)

This function needs, at a minimum, just two things: where and what. As in, *where* are we going to write our package files and *what* will we initially populate them with? We choose the directory *~/NMRpackage*, and will start with one of the functions from our script:

```
> setwd("~")
> package.skeleton("NMRpackage", c("readNMRData"))
Creating directories ...
Creating DESCRIPTION ...
Creating Read-and-delete-me ...
```

```
Saving functions and data ...
Making help files ...
Done.
Further steps are described in '/~NMRpackage/Read-and-delete-me'.
```

We now want to inform RStudio that we are working on a new project, allowing us to compartmentalize our session data and accompanying functions. A more detailed desciption of projects in RStudio is postponed to "Organizing Activities with Projects" on page 73, for now we note that we used the directory just created by package.skeleton.

After creating a new project, we refresh the Files browser to show us which files were created (Figure 4-3).

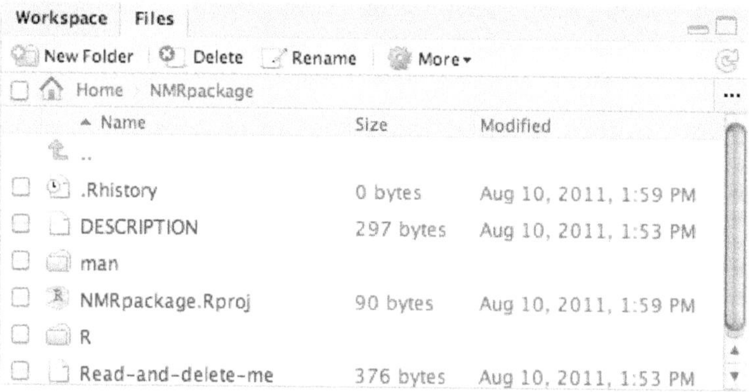

Figure 4-3. Directory structure after package.skeleton call

We see two unexpected files in the base directory and two subdirectories. We first investigate what is in the Read-and-delete-me by clicking on the link and reading. For now, nothing we need. It says to delete the file, so we oblige by selecting the file's checkbox and clicking the Delete toolbar button.

The DESCRIPTION file is used by R to organize its packages. Ours needs to be updated to reflect our package. Clicking the link opens the file in the code editor. Here we edit the Title: field and some others. Since our package will rely on the zoo and ggplot2 packages, we add those to the Depends field. This file is in dcf format with a keyword (the name before the colon) and value on one line. If you need more lines for the value, just give any additional lines some indented space, as was done for the "Description:" line (see Figure 4-4).

The R directory is where all the programming is done. In this directory we have the files containing our function definitions. We change our working directory (Ctrl+Shift+K), and the file browser updates to show this directory.

We see that the call to package.skeleton created a file named *readNMRData.R*, containing the definition of the one function we gave it. We could have one file per function,

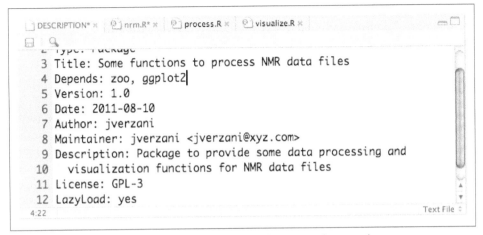

Figure 4-4. Editing the stock DESCRIPTION file template to match our package

but that will quickly get unwieldy. We could also put all our functions into one file—but again that gets bulky. A better strategy is to group similar functions together into a file. For now, we will create a file to hold our data-processing functions (*process.R*), and another file for our still-to-be-written visualization functions (*visualize.R*).

To rename our file through the `Files` browser, we select its checkbox and then click the `Rename` toolbar button. A dialog prompts us for the new name. We open this file for editing by clicking on its link. We then open our original script file (*one-big-script-file.R*, which isn't in our new project) by using the Open File toolbar button on the application's toolbar. We then proceed to use the magic wand to create functions `createZooObjects` and `createStateMatrix`. These are then copy-and-pasted into the appropriate file in the *R* directory.

RStudio has some facilities for navigating through a file full of functions. The "Go to file/function" search box in the main toolbar, allows one to quickly and conveniently navigate to all the functions in a project. For in-file navigation, in the lower-left corner of the code-editor component sits a label (Figure 4-5) that contains the line and column number, and next to that, a combobox that can be popped up to select a function to jump to.

```
35 createStateMatrix <- function (x) {
36  m       do call (                )
37  m   readNMRData              FALSE)
38 }      createZooObjects
39        createStateMatrix
40
39:1    createZooObjects
```

Figure 4-5. The function pop up allows you to quickly navigate to a function in a file containing many functions

We next open a new R Script (Shift+Ctrl+N or through the File menu) for holding any functions for visualization and add a function to use ggplot2 to make a graphic. We save the file and update our Files menu through its Refresh button.

Documenting Functions With roxygen2

The package.skeleton command makes the man subdirectory. In R, all exported functions must be documented in some file. Such files are written using R's Rd markup language. Looking at the man directory, we see that two files were made: *read-NMRData.Rd* (a stub for our function), and *NMRpackage-package.Rd* (a stub for documenting the entire package). We open up the latter and make the required changes —at a minimum, the lines that have paired double tildes are edited to match our idea of the package.

We could go on to edit the *readNMRData.Rd* template, but instead we will use the roxygen2 package to document our package's functions. Although R is organized around a workflow where one writes the function then documents it separately (presumably after the function is done), many other programming languages have facilities for writing in a *literate programming* style using inline documentation. Some R programmers are used to this functionality (it simplifies iterative function writing and documenting) and the roxygen2 package makes this feasible. For the modest demands of this package, it is an excellent choice.

Rd format has a number of required sections, and using roxygen2 does not eliminate the need for following that structure. All directives appear in comments (we use ##'). Keywords are prefaced with an at symbol (@). The main sections that are usually defined are a title (taken from the first line), an optional description (taken from the first paragraph), the function's arguments (defined through the @param tags), a description of the return value (@return), whether the function will be exported (@export), and, optionally some examples. R has tools to check that the right format is followed. In particular, it will catch if you have failed to document all the arguments or if you misname a section tag.

The Rd markup is fairly straightforward and is described in the *Writing R Extensions* manual. An example of a documented function is shown in Figure 4-6.

We can also create a NEWS file to keep track of changes between versions of the package. This may not be useful for this package, but if the package proves popular with our colleagues, a NEWS file will help them see what has happened with our package (Figure 4-7). The NEWS file is a plain-text file with a simple structure. We open it through the File > New menu, but this time select Text File. The code editor will present a different toolbar in this case, as it makes no sense to be able to source R code from this file.

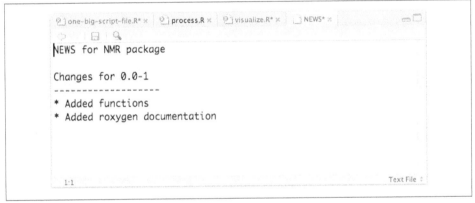

```
one-big-script-file.R* ×   process.R ×   visualize.R* ×
         Source on Save            ▼                                    Run          Source ▼
##' Make a times series plot using ggplot2
##'
##' @param x a possibly multidimensional zoo object
##' @return a ggplot object to be printed
##' @export
nmrTsPlot <- function(x) {
  if(all(class(x) != "zoo")) stop("x must be a zoo object")
  x.df <- data.frame(dates=index(x), coredata(x))
  x.df <- melt(x.df, id="dates", variable="value")
  names(x.df)[2] = "ID"
3:15    (Top Level)                                                    R Script
```

Figure 4-6. Illustration of using roxygen2 to document a function

```
one-big-script-file.R* ×   process.R ×   visualize.R* ×    NEWS* ×

NEWS for NMR package

Changes for 0.0-1
--------------------
* Added functions
* Added roxygen documentation




1:1                                                                   Text File
```

Figure 4-7. Editing a text file in the Source code editor shows that the toolbar is file-type dependent

The devtools Package

Testing a package can involve loading the package, testing it, making desired changes, then reloading the package. This workflow can get tedious—it can even involve closing and restarting R to flush residual changes. The devtools package is designed to make this task easier.

If it isn't installed, we can install it from CRAN using the Packages component (Figure 4-8). Click the Install Packages toolbar button and then type the desired package name into the dialog. (An auto-complete feature makes this easy.) Leaving the Install dependencies option checked will also install roxygen2 and the testthat package, if needed.

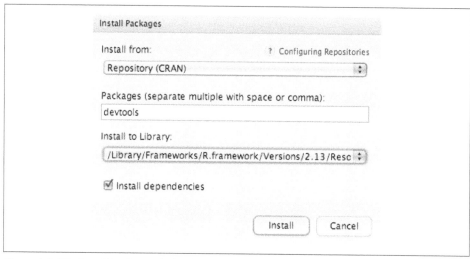

Figure 4-8. The Install Packages dialog for installing the devtools package

Rtools

Windows users will want to install RTools, a set of development tools for Windows maintained by D. Murdoch. The files are found at *http://cran.r-project.org/bin/windows/Rtools* .

The devtools package provides the load_all function to reload the package without having to restart R. To use it we define a package variable (pkg) pointing to the directory (an *".Rpackages"* file can be used to avoid this step), then load the code (Figure 4-9). The new functions do not appear in the Workspace browser, as they are stored in an environment just below the global workspace, but they do show up through RStudio's code-completion functionality.

We can try it out. In doing so, if we realize that we would like to change some function, no problem. We make the adjustment in the code editor, save the file, then reissue the command load_all(pkg).

For working with documentation, the devtools package has the document function (as in document(pkg)) to call roxygen2 to create the corresponding Rd files and show_news to view the NEWS file.

Package Data

We can add our testing commands in an example, but we will need to have some data to use when we distribute our package. We wrote readNMRData to accept any data file in the same format, as we imagine our colleagues using it with other data sets generated by the experiment. However, we can combine the data we have into the package for

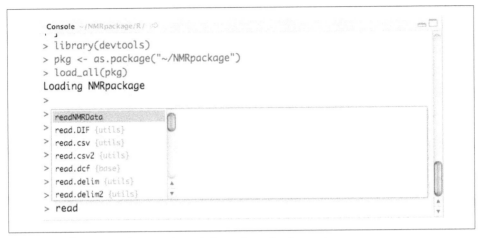

Figure 4-9. The commands to use devtools for package development

testing and example purposes. R has the `data` directory for including data in a package. This data should be in a format R can easily read in—ours isn't (it has a different separator and we need to skip every other line). So instead, we use the `inst` directory to create our own data directory. We call this `sampledata` (not `data`, as this would interfere with the `data` directory that R processes automatically). We create the needed directories with the `New Folder` toolbar button in the `Files` browser.

How you get the package data file into this folder depends on how you are using RStudio. If you are using the desktop version, you simply copy the file over using your usual method (e.g., Finder, command line, Windows Explorer). If you are using the server version, then this won't work. In that case, the `Files` component has an additional `Upload` toolbar button to allow you to upload your file. This button summons a dialog that allows you to browse for a file or a *zip* archive of many files (Figure 4-10).

Upload Files

Target directory:

🏠 Home

File to upload:

(Choose File) No file chosen

TIP: To upload multiple files or a directory, create a zip file. The zip file will be automatically expanded after upload.

[OK]   [Cancel]

Figure 4-10. Dialog for uploading a file to the server (server usage only)

Package Examples

R documentation files have the option of an "examples" section, where one would usually see documentation of example usage of the function(s). This is a very good idea, as it gives the user a sample template to build on. In Figure 4-11, we see sample code added to our `readNMRData` function's documentation.

```
##' @export
##' @examples
##' ## f <- "~/NMRpackage/inst/sampledata/degas.txt"
##' f <- system.file("sampledata","degas.txt", package="NMRpackag
##' a <- readNMRData(f)
##' b <- createZooObjects(a)
##' m <-   createStateMatrix(b)
##' nmrTsPlot(m[, 1:4])
readNMRData <- function (f) {
```

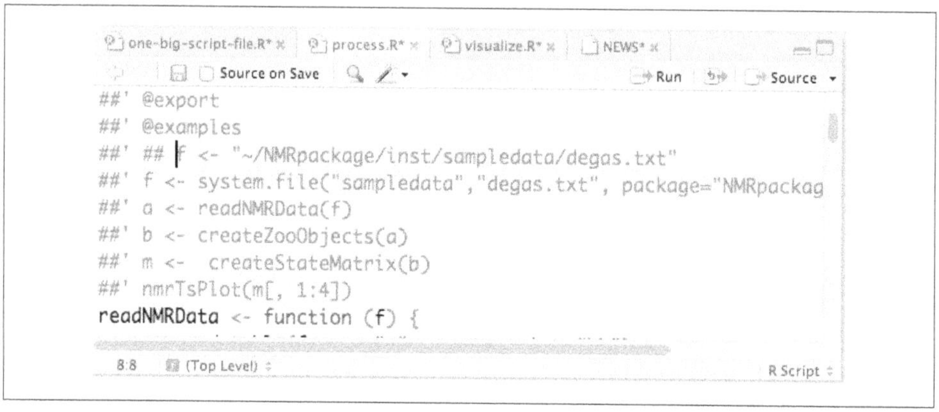

Figure 4-11. Adding an example to a function's documentation with roxygen2

For an installed package, examples can be run by the user through the `example` function. During development with `devtools`, the programmer can use the `run_examples` function.

Adding Tests

Although examples will typically be run during package development, it is a good practice to include tests of the package's core functions as well. Tests serve a different purpose than examples. Well-designed tests can help find bugs introduced by changes to functions—a not uncommon event. The `devtools` package can run tests (through `testthat`) that appear in the `inst/tests` subdirectory of the package.

Building and Installing the Package

Packages can be checked for issues, built for distribution and installed for subsequent usage. RStudio does not have any features for performing such, but all can be done within devtools, or from a shell outside of the R process. For example, a UNIX or Mac OS X user could run:

```
> system("cd ~; R CMD build NMRpackage")
```

We could replace `build` with `CHECK` to check our package for consistency with R's expectations. Though checking isn't required for sharing a package with colleagues, a package distributed on CRAN should pass the check phase cleanly. Checking is a good thing in any case.

Installing locally built packages can be done from the *Install Packages* dialog by selecting the option to install from a `Package Archive File (.tgz)`.

The `devtools` package provides the functions `check`, `build`, and `install` for performing these three basic tasks.

For Windows users, the *WinBuilder* project (*http://win-builder.R-project.org*) is a web service that can be used to create packages. Otherwise, building R packages under Windows is made easier using the `Rtools` bundle mentioned earlier.

CHAPTER 5

Programming R with RStudio

Programming R involves the writing, editing, debugging, and documenting of functions; working with function files; and packaging functions for wider distribution. In this chapter we look at some components of RStudio that simplify these and other tasks.

Source Code Editor

Recall that RStudio leverages numerous web technologies. A major one is the Ace code editor (*ace.ajax.org*) for editing functions and files. Ace is written in JavaScript, which allows all necessary computations to be done in the client, thereby avoiding numerous calls to the server. This is important, as an editor for an IDE must do many things well and *quickly*, such as:

- File-type specific syntax highlighting
- Automatic code indentation
- Parenthesis matching
- Working with many documents simultaneously
- Working with large documents
- Working with different languages

While not as feature-rich as some editors—say, the Emacs editor that powers ESS— the Ace editor in the RStudio framework is still quite able and easy to work with. The component uses tabs to organize the files and provides toolbars and other means to issue common commands quickly.

Basics

The action to open a new file in the Source code editor is presented in many different ways: under the File > New menu item, the leftmost toolbar button in the application-wide toolbar pops up the choices, and the keyboard shortcut opens an R file. The code editor can open text files of various types. The menu items include an R Script, a Text File, an Sweave Document, and a TeX Document. In Figure 5-1, we show how the component's toolbar adjusts to provide file-type specific actions.

Similarly, existing files can be opened through a menu item, a toolbar button or a keyboard shortcut. In addition, active links in the Files browser can be used to open a file. A selection of recently opened files is available through the application toolbar and the menu.

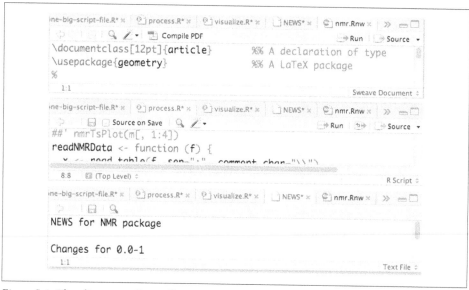

Figure 5-1. The edit pane toolbar is file-type sensitive. Here we see scripts, Sweave files, and text files

Files that have unsaved changes are marked with an asterisk next to their name in their tab's label. For such files, the standard Save and Save as... actions are also accessed through the menu bar, the application-wide toolbar, or keyboard shortcuts. In addition, the Save with Encoding... menu item can be used to specify an encoding for the file when saving. As a convenience, the Save All action is available through the menu bar or application-wide toolbar.

A file can be closed by clicking on the "x" icon in the tab for a file, through a menu item, or through the appropriate keyboard shortcut, Ctrl+W or Cmd+W. (Except for the Chrome browser under Mac OS X, where Ctrl+Shift+L is used, as the other shortcut is used to close the browser window.) If there are unsaved changes, you will be asked whether you want to save the work.

The editor allows one to have many different files open at once. When a moderate-sized number of files are open, one navigates between them by clicking on the appropriate tab. There are shortcuts for cycling through the tabs (Next, Previous, First, Last). As well, the widget provides a means to select a tab to jump to. This is especially useful if there are so many tabs that their labels don't fit in the allocated width (Figure 5-2). This widget provides a drop-down menu and a search box.

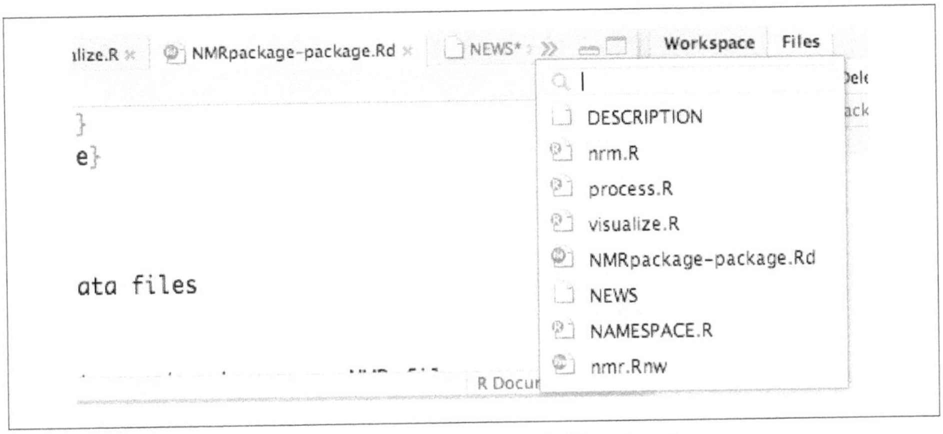

Figure 5-2. RStudio provides a convenient means to switch files when there are many open

The Find and Replace menu item implements a search through the currently opened file. When run through a web browser, the browser's search function may search through the entire page. There is no such feature in the desktop version. (Therefore, each component has its own search bar.)

Instead of a search dialog, the Ace editor produces an unobtrusive pop-down bar in the code editor (Figure 5-3) that allows a user to find (and replace) strings of text. Checkboxes allow one to restrict the search by case-matching or widen it using regular expressions (see ?regex). The Find button marches through the document moving to each new match, wrapping at the end of the document. The Replace and All buttons control how to replace the found text with an alternative.

Figure 5-3. The panel that appears when searching in the code editor

The Editing pane of the Options dialog (Figure 3-4) has options for adjusting the behavior of the editor. In that screenshot, you can see we have turned off the automatic insertion of matching parentheses and quotes, but otherwise the defaults are to our particular taste.

There is also an option to toggle line numbering. When this option is on, line numbers appear along the left margin. In either case, down in the lower left corner of the code-editor window is a label (Figure 5-5) listing the current line number and position of the cursor.

File synchronization

When a file is opened in the editor, it is not locked and may be modified through some other process, such as being altered by your favorite editor. RStudio will monitor changes in the underlying file and propagate them back.

Keyboard shortcuts

In Table 5-1, we list several keyboard shortcuts provided by RStudio for basic editing needs. There are the standard operating system shortcuts for things like cut, copy, and paste; undo and redo, etc. In addition, some, such as the "yank" commands, come from the Emacs world.

Table 5-1. Selected keyboard shortcuts for console and source usage

Action	Windows and Linux	Mac OS X
Undo	Ctrl+Z	Command+Z
Redo	Ctrl+Shift+Z	Command+Shift+Z
Cut	Ctrl+X	Command+X
Copy	Ctrl+C	Command+C
Paste	Ctrl+V	Command+V
Select All	Ctrl+A	Command+A
Jump to Word	Ctrl+Left/Right	Option+Left/Right
Jump to Start/End	Ctrl+Home/End or Ctrl+Up/Down	Command+Home/End or Command+Up/Down
Delete Line	Ctrl+D	Command+D
Select	Shift+[Arrow]	Shift+[Arrow]
Select Word	Ctrl+Shift+Left/Right	Option+Shift+Left/Right
Select to Line Start	Shift+Home	Command+Shift+Left or Shift+Home
Select to Line End	Shift+End	Command+Shift+Right or Shift+End
Select Page Up/Down	Shift+PageUp/PageDown	Shift+PageUp/Down
Select to Start/End	Ctrl+Shift+Home/End or Shift+Alt+Up/Down	Command+Shift+Up/Down

Action	Windows and Linux	Mac OS X
Delete Word Left	Ctrl+Backspace	Option+Backspace or Ctrl+Option+Backspace
Delete Word Right	n/a	Option+Delete
Delete to Line End	n/a	Ctrl+K
Delete to Line Start	n/a	Option+Backspace
Indent	Tab (at beginning of line)	Tab (at beginning of line)
Outdent	Shift+Tab	Shift+Tab
Yank line up to cursor	Ctrl+U	Ctrl+U
Yank line after cursor	Ctrl+K	Ctrl+K
Insert currently yanked text	Ctrl+Y	Ctrl+Y
Insert assignment operator	Alt+-	Option+-

R Programming Features

RStudio augments the Ace editor with some R-specific conveniences.

Syntax highlighting

Syntax highlighting is implemented by RStudio for files related to R development (Figure 5-4). Highlighting provides separate colors for keywords, functions, and other objects, so they are readily identified. There isn't much for the R programmer to do here except enjoy the benefits.

```
1  AND <- function(x) UseMethod("AND")
2
3  AND.default <- function(x) {
4    Reduce("&", x)
5  }
6
7  AND.matrix <- function(x) {
8    AND(as.data.frame(x))
9  }
```

Figure 5-4. Illustration of syntax highlighting (function keyword in blue, "AND" string in green), automatic indenting of block expressions (inside {}, say), and parenthesis matching (the cursor is at last }, and the matching { is highlighted)

Having comments in a different color from the text makes them much more readable and at the same time unobtrusive. Working with comments in R involves simply placing a pound (#) symbol somewhere on a line, so that the text to the right is ignored by the interpreter. (There are no Emacs-like comment conventions for repeated pound symbols.) Comments can be added to an entire block of text through the Comment/Uncomment Lines menu item (under the magic wand). Simply select the text, and this action will toggle the comment state.

Bracket matching

The R syntax requires several matching delimiters, such as matching square brackets for vector extraction, matching parentheses for functions, matching braces for blocks of commands, and matching quotes for strings. RStudio has two means to assist the bookkeeping required for this demand. It can be done either automatically through the insertion of a matching bracket when the opening one is given—or if this is turned off, through highlighting. A setting in the *Editing* pane of the Options dialog is used to adjust the behavior.

Automatic indenting

Within code blocks delimited by curly braces, it can be useful to have indenting to quickly identify the level of nesting. This is quite common—for instance, a simple for loop within a function body has this nesting. RStudio automatically indents the next line after the Enter key is pressed. In addition, pressing the Tab key when the cursor is at the start of a line will indent that line.

For indenting the current line or formatting a selected region, the magic wand has the action "Reindent Lines" (also Ctrl+I).

Compare Readability without Indenting and Spacing

To see the advantage of improved readability, compare these two coding styles—the latter uses some typical R programming conventions (the arrow over the equals sign, space around operators and after commas, and indenting to indicate nesting):

```
mlp=function(theta,data)
{
n=length(data)
mu=theta[,1]; sigma=exp(theta[,2])
val=0*mu
for (i in 1:n)
{
val=val+dnorm(data[i],mean=mu,sd=sigma,log=TRUE)
}
val=val+dnorm(mu,mean=10,sd=20,log=TRUE)
return(val)
}
```

---

and:

```
mlp <- function(theta, data) {
  n <- length(data)
  mu <- theta[, 1]
  sigma <- exp(theta[, 2])
  val <- 0*mu
  for (i in 1:n) {
    val <- val + dnorm(data[i], mean=mu, sd=sigma, log=TRUE)
  }
  val <- val + dnorm(mu, mean=10, sd=20, log=TRUE)
  return(val)
}
```

Code completion and usage information

The Tab key completion features of the console (see "Tab Completion" on page 29) are also present when working with the code editor. To review, a token is the last word or fragment in a given line. When the Tab key is pressed, the completions for this token and its context are analyzed:

Object completion
> When the token is a partially typed object name, the candidates for completion include objects available in the global workspace. If possible, the completion provides a summary for each candidate from R's help mechanism.

Argument completion
> When the token is the opening of a function, the candidates include a list and a description of the function's arguments from the function's help page.

Argument or object completion
> When the token is at a function argument and a start is given, the completion includes matching argument names and matching objects, as either could be given.

String completion
> Candidates for string completion are the filenames in the current working directory.

Extract function

In our case study, we took on the task of converting a script of commands into a package, creating several functions in the process. The Extract Function feature (the magic wand toolbar button) helps facilitate this, trying to create a function from the currently selected lines in an R script. To use this feature, highlight the commands that you want to include in the definition of the function, then invoke the magic wand. A dialog gathers a function name, then the selected commands are parsed to make a guess as to what the argument to the function should be.

Run or source commands

We mentioned in "R Script Files" on page 27 that one can select parts of an R script in the code editor and send the commands to the R interpreter. The Ctrl+Enter and Ctrl +Shift+Enter shortcuts make this process very convenient (the full list was provided in Table 3-2).

Navigation

As projects grow, it is typical to have multiple files, each containing many functions grouped in some manner. Being able to navigate quickly within a file and among files becomes a welcome convenience.

Jump to function

In addition to searching through a file, RStudio has features for navigating among the functions in an R script file. The "Jump to function" action is invoked through a menu item, a keyboard shortcut (Ctrl-Alt-Up), or a pop up located in the bottom status bar of the code editor window (Figure 5-5). Selecting a function moves the cursor to the beginning of the function's definition.

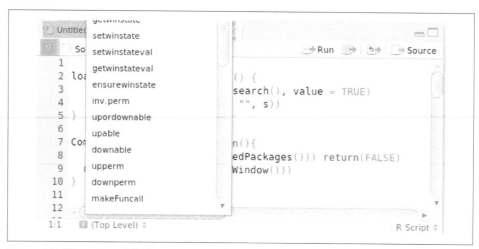

Figure 5-5. Illustration of the function pop up feature to jump to function's definition

Go to file/function

To quickly navigate between files and functions within a project, RStudio provides the tremendously useful `Go to File/Function` action with the shortcut *Ctrl+.* . The application's tool bar always shows this, and the shortcut moves the focus to this entry area. This action provides a text entry box where a user can type either a function name or file name. Automatic completion candidates are given from both, so one can quickly and conveniently jump around within a project. The files and functions that make up a project are monitored for changes, so even changes external to RStudio can be tracked.

Generic Functions in R

As mentioned, user-written functions are how R is extended. With over 3,000 packages and countless other uses, there needs to be some means of bringing order to this. R has a notion of a *generic function* that allows the same function name to be used in different contexts. The role of the generic function is to consult the arguments it is given and dispatch (or call) the appropriate function (in this context, the function is called a method). This allows the user to use just one name for many different—yet similar—tasks. A prime example is the `plot` function, where many different types of plots are produced, depending on the class of the first argument.

The `plot` function is an *S3* generic function. Such functions dispatch on the class of the first argument, and methods can be written using the naming convention `generic.class name`. (In Figure 3-5 we see several methods for the `mean` function listed.)

There are also *S4* generics that dispatch, possibly, on the class of each argument given, not just the first. These are registered (rather than just named appropriately) through the `setMethod` function.

Reference classes are related, though the methods therein do not use generics.

As of recent versions of RStudio, these methods do appear in the "Go To File/Function" list.

The File Browser

The `Files` browser (Figure 5-6) displays the files and subdirectories of a given directory. The refresh toolbar button will refresh this display, if clicked. There are just a few actions. Clicking on a subdirectory will load the contents of that directory into the file browser. Clicking on a file will open an editor or viewer for that file. For text files with certain extensions, this will be the source-code editor. Otherwise, this will be a system program if the source-code editor is not appropriate. For example, a *.pdf* file will open in a PDF viewer on the desktop; or from the browser (server version), in a new window; whereas a *.doc* file will open in Microsoft Word (or the associated program for the MIME type) on the desktop, but will be downloaded when run from the browser.

By selecting one or more files through the checkboxes on the left, one can initiate actions to delete, rename, copy, or move the file(s) through actions available from the toolbar buttons. One can create new folders through the `New Folder` toolbar button. If these actions are not sufficient, in the desktop version, the `More > Show Folder In New Window` toolbar item will invoke the system file manager for the directory.

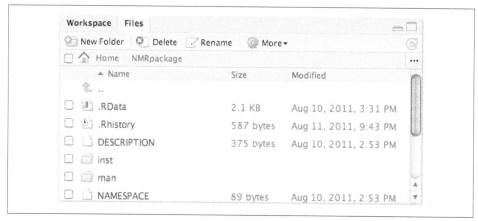

Figure 5-6. The Files browser showing a directory listing from a package with a mix of files and sub-directories

File upload

For server usage, there is a toolbar button to initiate a file upload. This is similar to attaching a file to an email, a reasonable analogy, as you may also be restricted from uploading files that are too large.

Debugging R Code in RStudio

R provides some useful tools for debugging R code, summarized online at *http://www.stats.uwo.ca/faculty/murdoch/software/debuggingR/debug.shtml*. These tools allow R users to investigate errors, step through functions, insert debugging code, etc. Although RStudio currently doesn't have additional integration with R's debugging tools, the RStudio console does work with these functions.

Package Maintenance

R uses *packages* to extend itself and RStudio provides the `Packages` browser to make it effortless to load, install, update, and/or delete packages in the library of packages.

In Figure 5-7 we show a screenshot. Each installed package is shown with a description derived from the package's `DESCRIPTION` file. In addition, for each package there is:

- A checkbox to load (`require`) or unload (`detach`) the package
- An active link to open the help page index of the package
- A delete icon to uninstall the package from the library

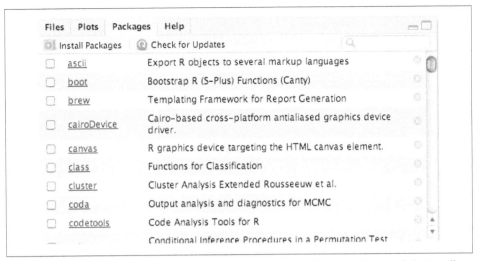

Figure 5-7. Screenshot of the Packages component, used for loading a package and the installing, deleting, and updating of the library of packages

The `Packages` browser toolbar has a `Check for Updates` button, which is used to see if any packages have pending updates. The dialog this opens is similar to Figure 5-8, where those packages with possible updates on a system are listed. One simply selects the packages to update and then presses the `Install Updates` button. From there, RStudio calls `install.packages` to download the new packages from a repository to install.

	Package	Installed	Available	NEWS
☐	KernSmooth	2.23-4	2.23-6	
☐	RColorBrewer	1.0-2	1.0-5	
☐	RGtk2	2.20.12	2.20.14	
☐	RJSONIO	0.7-2	0.7-3	
☐	RgoogleMaps	1.1.9.7	1.1.9.8	
☐	WMCapacity	0.9.6.0	0.9.6.5	
☐	boot	1.2-43	1.3-2	
☐	brew	1.0-4	1.0-6	
☐	cluster	1.13.3	1.14.0	
☐	colorspace	1.0-1	1.1-0	

Figure 5-8. Dialog showing packages that have available updates

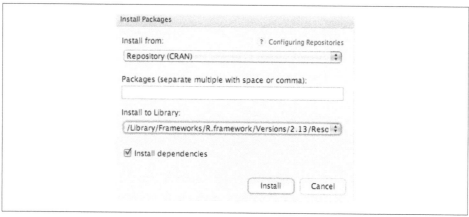

Figure 5-9. Dialog to install a package; you must specify what, from where, and to where

You can install new packages through the dialog that opens when you press the Install Packages toolbar button (Figure 5-9). In the figure, the "Install dependencies" checkbox is selected, instructing `install.packages` to also download and install any packages that the desired ones depend on. In addition, several other things must be specified:

Which package
> Which package (or packages) to install is specified in the middle text entry box titled "Packages". There are over 3,000 packages, so presenting them all in a list is a poor interface. Rather than browsing through the available choices, the text entry box has an auto-completion feature that shows available packages matching the currently typed text token.

Which repository
> Packages are hosted on CRAN and elsewhere. CRAN is a system of repositories that mirror a central repository in Austria. One must choose a specific one from which to download the files. RStudio will keep track of this choice. If this has not been done, a dialog to choose a CRAN mirror will appear before the Install Packages dialog. One may also choose to install from a local "Package Archive File." The help-page link for "Configuring Repositories" shows the manual page for `setRepo sitories`, which spells out how one specifies non-CRAN repositories, such as those for the BioConductor project.

Which directory
> R will look for installed packages in several places (e.g., system-wide locations and user-specific locations) but won't scan the entire hard drive. When installing a package, one must specify which places will be checked. The dialog provides a combobox to select a Library directory. The available choices are determined by consulting the `.libPaths` function. This function both returns the places where packages are looked for and allows one to append to this search list. The server

version allows a choice of a directory in the user's home directory, as otherwise certain permissions would be required. For the desktop version, if a local, user-only spot is desired, one can call the `.libPaths` function from the console to provide the desired location.

Organizing Activities with Projects

RStudio allows one to organize their work and files into projects, with each project having its own associated directory and global workspace. This is a fantastic feature for keeping your different workflows separate. Projects can also take advantage of RStudio's version control features ("Version Control with RStudio" on page 75), giving you confidence that you can recover from erroneous changes and easily collaborate with others.

When a project is opened, much of the past session is restored. The project's profile, data and history files are restored, the working directory is reset, the previously opened files are reopened, and RStudio's layout settings are set to match when the project was last closed.

The upper-right corner of the main application toolbar holds the project selector. This shows the currently selected project (if any)—and more importantly, provides a convenient way to to create a new project, switch to a different project, close the current project, or adjust options for the current project. These actions are also found under the `Project` menu where there is also the additional option to open a project in a new window. This is used to open more than one project simultaneously. To select a project, one browses for the *proj* file created with the project.

Creating a new project is straightforward. The wizard for doing so first asks (Figure 5-10) if you want to start with a new directory, use a new directory, or check out a project which is using version control. Selecting the new directory option requires (Figure 5-11) that one specifies a name, a directory and indicate if version control is to be used.

Figure 5-12 shows how after creating a new project with a Git repository, the tabbed `Git` pane appears, as well as some new files are created in the project's directory.

While one is working within a project, any changes to the workspace are stored with the project (unless this behavior is changed through the `Project Options` dialog). The files in the directory are indexed to look for changes, allowing the "Go to file/function" search box to be used to quickly navigate to any defined function in the project.

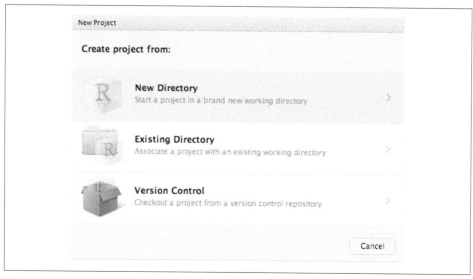

Figure 5-10. There are three ways to create a new project depending on what has already been done

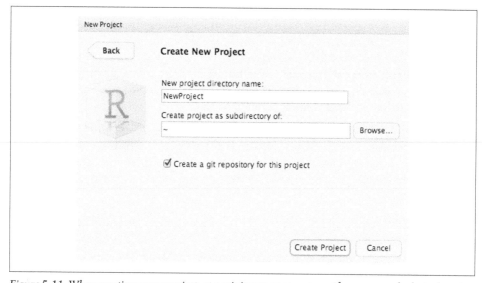

Figure 5-11. When creating a new project, at a minimum one must specify a name and select a location

Figure 5-12. In creating a new project with a git repository, RStudio displays a Git pane and creates a few auxiliary files

Version Control with RStudio

RStudio's project infrastructure allows a project to be integrated in with one of two popular version control systems, Git and Subversion. Both are widely used: e.g., the R project uses Subversion, whereas RStudio uses Git. Version control systems provide two very useful features:

- They keep a history of changes to a file and allow one to browse or rollback to previous versions. This is similar to what is provided by Apple Computer's popular Time Machine software for backups.

- Version control systems allow multiple users to work on the same project without stepping on each other's toes. This is similar to how the Track Changes feature of Microsoft Word allows groups to work collaboratively on a Word document, but better, as changes can be made by all parties at the same time and the version control system merges the changes together. This only requires intervention when there are conflicts.

Getting started with version control

RStudio makes the cost of using version control so minimal that it is highly recommended for any new project. Before getting started, you must have the underlying version control tools installed on your system: one of the open-source projects, Git or Subversion. We will focus on Git in the following section.

If Git is not installed, the main Git website (*http://www.git-scm.com/*) points to downloads for both Windows and Mac OS X users and a source download for Linux users, if the underlying distribution doesn't provide a pre-compiled solution. Installation is typically straightforward. If needed, more details on installation (along with much more not touched on here) are given in the Git Community Book, *http://book.git-scm.com/*.

Using Git to keep a history of changes

When a project is under version control, then that software will track changes to the files in its repository. There are different possible file states as compared to those recognized in the repository: a file can not be in the repository, the file can have been deleted from the repository, a file can be deleted locally but still in the repository, or the file can be modified from that in the repository. RStudio tracks these differences and displays them in its Git pane. In Figure 5-12, there are two new files on the file system that are not in the repository. In Figure 5-13, we illustrate how the Git pane and the Files pane account for files in a different manner, depending on their state. This information is equivalent to the command git status.

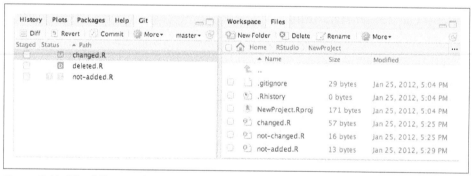

Figure 5-13. The differences between the repository and the file system are illustrated here. The changed.R file shows a modified icon in the Git pane; the deleted.R file has been removed from the file system so it does not appear in the Files pane, but does have a deleted icon in the Git pane; and the not-added.R file is new and has not been added to the repository, so shows up as a file, but shows an unknown status in the Git pane. Other files in the repository appearing in the Files pane do not appear in the Git pane, as no changes have been made

The Staged column in the Git pane has checkboxes that instruct Git to index that file to be included in the repository during the next commit, providing the functionality of the command git add.

Putting staged changes into the repository is called "committing." The Commit icon in the Git panes toolbar opens the Review Changes dialog to assist with this task. In Figure 5-14, we show the dialog for committing three changes. In the upper-right corner of the dialog is an area to leave a message associated with the commit. Though leaving a message is technically optional, one should strive to give short but informative messages, as they are very helpful when auditing file changes. Selecting the History view in the dialog shows previously left messages (along with much more).

In the top-left corner of the dialog appears a list of the files that differ from the repository. Again, one can adjust whether a file is staged or not. The currently selected file has its differences between the repository and the file system highlighted, allowing a quick review of what is new.

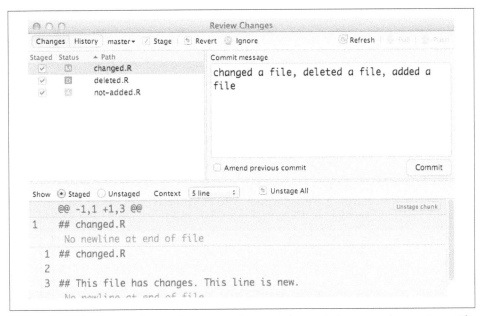

Figure 5-14. The Review Changes dialog is used to commit staged changes to the repository. The upper-right area allows one to associate a message with the commit and the lower part shows the differences between the selected file in the upper-left listing and the file in the repository

If you change your mind on a commit, you can check out an old copy of the file. The Git command git checkout allows this. This isn't directly provided by the interface. However, RStudio provides a convenient way to issue arbitrary Git commands through a built-in Git shell. The shell is raised through the menu item More > Shell.... The command git checkout HEAD^ deleted.R would then check out the file that was deleted and allow you to stage it for reinclusion.

Git allows one to make "branches" of a project that can be reintegrated back into the main project. This is a convenient way to experiment with changes without worrying about the impact on the current project along the way. To make a branch, the Git command `git branch branch_name` is used. RStudio makes it trivial to choose among the current branches, as next to the refresh icon in the `Git` pane's toolbar is a selector to switch between branches. In Figure 5-15, we show the `History` view after creating a branch and adding a new file *experimental.R* to it. This file is in the new branch but not the old. To merge a branch back into the master, the `git merge branch_name` command is used.

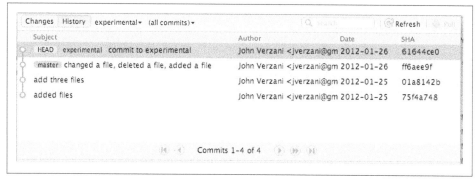

Figure 5-15. The History view showing a branch, experimental, with a file added to it

Collaborating with Git

One of the great features of Git is the ability to collaborate with others on a project. There are two concepts: we "pull" changes made by others, and we "push" our changes back to others. When we check out a project from a Git repository, RStudio activates these options in the `Review Changes` dialog. Figure 5-16 shows the output of clicking `Pull` after our local copy of a repository requested updates made on the repository hosted at *www.github.com*, an enormously popular hosting site for Git projects. When connecting to such sites, it may be necessary to authenticate, typically through SSH. RStudio includes the necessary platform files to make this work similarly on all platforms.

When collaborating, there is always the possibility that you or your colleagues may be working on the same thing. In particular, you may both have made changes to the same file. While resolving different edits is often possible without intervention, this is not always the case. When it is not, the `merge` command of Git reports back to RStudio the actions that need to be taken. In Figure 5-17, we see such a report.

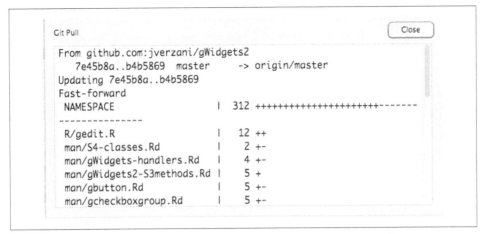

Figure 5-16. A review of the modifications after a Pull request provided by RStudio

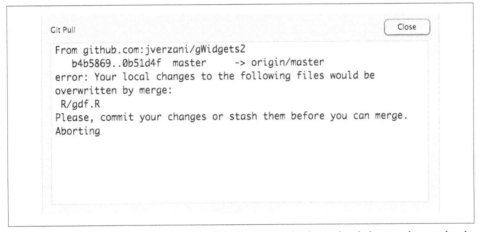

Figure 5-17. When a pull request is made, RStudio reports back any local changes that need to be addressed before the request can be completed. In this case, the suggestion is to commit or stash the local change

Case Study: Report Generation using Sweave

In two previous case studies, we saw how RStudio can be used in an interactive manner, and how RStudio can be used to write the functions that compose a package. In this example, we look at how RStudio can be used to write reports where we automatically mix R output into the report. If our data changes, we just rerun it. This allows us to keep all our numbers and references in sync. It allows us to create reproducible research, as the document contains all the code needed to produce it. The main tool is *Sweave*, a literate programming tool for R that can "weave" R commands into a document, formatted with marked-up text. (Typically, but not necessarily, this is *LaTeX*, which we illustrate here—but there are other implementations for Open Office, asciidoc, etc.)

Knitr

The *knitr* package is a newer alternative to *Sweave*.

A vignette is a longer form of documentation for R packages and is usually written using Sweave. For our naked mole rat package, we have provided our colleagues with functions and documented them using `roxygen2`. Now we see how to write a vignette, allowing us to mix in our observations and insights along with use cases and detail about the functionality we have provided.

Vignettes can simply be a Sweave file saved in the *inst/doc* subdirectory of the package. When a package is "checked," the vignette's code is executed; when a package is "built," a *pdf* file is created for distribution with the package. There is some control over this—for more detail, see the section *Writing Package Vignettes* in the *Writing R Extensions* manual.

To begin, we open a file *nmr.Rnw* after creating the *doc* directory through the `Files` browser. RStudio's code-editor `File > New` menu has an option for a new `Sweave Document`, which we select. The code-editor toolbar and status bar are specific to the document type. For an *Sweave* document, which mixes R code and *LaTex* markup, it makes sense to allow the user to run commands in the console, so that option is still present. There is also a new `Compile PDF` button, which, when clicked, initiates the process of calling `Sweave` to replace the R commands with their output in a new file (the "weaving") and then calls R's `texi2dvi` function to create a *pdf* file. (This all assumes a working *LaTeX* is installed on your machine. If *LaTeX* is installed but a warning appears, its path may need to be specified.)

Figure 5-18 shows the code editor opened to a vignette. The lower-right corner indicates that it is editing an `Sweave Document`, and syntax highlighting is present both for the R code and the *LaTeX* text.

LaTeX is a markup language (the lingua franca of mathematicians) too complicated to describe here, but certainly not impossible to learn. It really helps to start with a basic template, such as this (*LaTeX* uses the percent sign for a comment character):

```
\documentclass[12pt]{article}        %% A declaration of type
\usepackage{geometry}                %% A LaTeX package
%
%\VignetteIndexEntry{Using the NMRpackage} %% Meta data lines
%\VignettePackage{NMRpackage}
%\VignetteDepends{zoo}
%
\title{NMRpackage}                   %% A LaTeX macro call
\author{John Verzani}
```

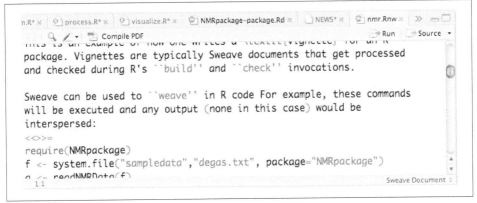

Figure 5-18. RStudio's code editor editing an Sweave file, as indicated in the lower-right corner

```
%
\begin{document}              %% Latex is between begin/end document
\maketitle                    %% Call a macro to make title
%
% ... Insert text here ...
%
\end{document}                %% End the document
```

The template shows how *LaTeX* calls commands (\maketitle) and uses begin/end environment pairs to mark larger sections of text.

The integration of R with *LaTeX* is done in two ways:

Code chunks

Code chunks are one or more commands to be executed, wrapped within tags beginning with <<>>= and ending with @. Within the <<>>, one can place directives to adjust what happens:

- With no directives, the code is echoed back with the output interspersed
- To name a block of code, the first directive should be a name (other arguments are in the form key=value). When named, this output can then be referred to through <<name>>.
- To suppress the code being echoed back, use echo=FALSE.
- To suppress the code being evaluated, use eval=FALSE.
- To suppress the results being included, use results=hide.
- To have *LaTeX* process the output (as opposed to having it included verbatim), use results=tex.
- To include a figure in the code, use fig=TRUE. For lattice graphics, one also needs to call print on the graph object.

Inline code

An R session inline; the expression can refer to variables defined in previous chunks.

For example, the following text would create a new section and a graphic:

```
\section{Making a plot}
The package provides the \texttt{nmrTsPlot} function to make a time series
graph using the \texttt{ggplot2} package. For example,
<<nmrTsPlot, fig=TRUE>>=
f <- system.file("sampledata","degas.txt", package="NMRpackage")
a <- readNMRData(f)
b <- createZooObjects(a)
m <- createStateMatrix(b)
out <- nmrTsPlot(m[, 1:4])
print(out)
@
```

Tables are straightforward, but can be tedious to typeset in *LaTeX*. Conveniently, one can use R to convert a rectangular object (matrix or data frame) to a table, using the add-on `xtable` package.

In the following we make a matrix, d, that holds the number of times that mole *i* is in the same chamber as mole *j*, by looping over the rows of the state matrix using `apply`. Then we use `xtable` to create the table. The `echo=FALSE` argument suppresses the R code, and `results=tex` is used to indicate that this output should be processed as *LaTeX* code:

```
<<makeTable, echo=FALSE>>=
n <- 8
d <- matrix(integer(n^2), nrow=n)
ind <- combn(1:n, 2)
f <- function(r) {
  apply(ind, 2, function(ij) {
    i <- ij[1]; j <- ij[2]
    x <- r[i] == r[j]
    if(!is.na(x))
      d[j,i] <<- d[i,j] <<- d[i, j] + as.numeric(x)
  })
}

out <- apply(m[, 1:n], 1, f)
diag(d) <- "-"
@

<<echo=FALSE, results=tex>>=
require(xtable)
out <- xtable(d, caption="Number of events mole rat $i$ is in same chamber as mole rat
$j$")
print(out)
@
```

To create a pdf file from our vignette, we click the `Compile PDF` toolbar button. This calls the `compilePdf` function provided by RStudio (which delegates to `texi2dvi` from the `tools` package). (Or, if using `devtools`, the `build_vignettes` function is available.) RStudio can also process plain *LaTeX* files; the process is identical. If the file extension matches one of the common extensions for weaving (*Rnw*, *Snw*, *nw*), Sweave is called first, then `texidvi`.

When an *Rnw* file is compiled, R first produces a *tex* file with the R commands interspersed, then *LaTeX* is run on this file. Doing so creates a number of files including a *pdf* file containing the output (if successful), a *log* file listing warnings and errors (if present), and perhaps others (e.g., an *aux* file). Most of these may be safely deleted, as they will be regenerated if needed.

If successful, the *pdf* file can be opened in a native viewer, or one can click on its link in the `Files` browser. If unsuccessful, one peruses the console output or the *log* file to find the errors.

About the Author

John Verzani is a longtime R user and author of *Using R for Introductory Statistics* (CRC, 2004) and with Michael Lawrence, *Programming GUIs in R* (CRC, forthcoming). He is a Professor and Chair in the Department of Mathematics at CUNY's College of Staten Island.

Get even more for your money.

Join the O'Reilly Community, and register the O'Reilly books you own. It's free, and you'll get:

- $4.99 ebook upgrade offer
- 40% upgrade offer on O'Reilly print books
- Membership discounts on books and events
- Free lifetime updates to ebooks and videos
- Multiple ebook formats, DRM FREE
- Participation in the O'Reilly community
- Newsletters
- Account management
- 100% Satisfaction Guarantee

Signing up is easy:

1. **Go to: oreilly.com/go/register**
2. **Create an O'Reilly login.**
3. **Provide your address.**
4. **Register your books.**

Note: English-language books only

To order books online:
oreilly.com/store

For questions about products or an order:
orders@oreilly.com

To sign up to get topic-specific email announcements and/or news about upcoming books, conferences, special offers, and new technologies:
elists@oreilly.com

For technical questions about book content:
booktech@oreilly.com

To submit new book proposals to our editors:
proposals@oreilly.com

O'Reilly books are available in multiple DRM-free ebook formats. For more information:
oreilly.com/ebooks

O'REILLY®

Spreading the knowledge of innovators   oreilly.com

The information you need, when and where you need it.

With Safari Books Online, you can:

Access the contents of thousands of technology and business books

- Quickly search over 7000 books and certification guides
- Download whole books or chapters in PDF format, at no extra cost, to print or read on the go
- Copy and paste code
- Save up to 35% on O'Reilly print books
- **New!** Access mobile-friendly books directly from cell phones and mobile devices

Stay up-to-date on emerging topics before the books are published

- Get on-demand access to evolving manuscripts.
- Interact directly with authors of upcoming books

Explore thousands of hours of video on technology and design topics

- Learn from expert video tutorials
- Watch and replay recorded conference sessions

Spreading the knowledge of innovators   safari.oreilly.com

Milton Keynes UK
Ingram Content Group UK Ltd.
UKHW031055061024
449279UK00007B/163